Advance Praise for

When we think of Al and Gloria, ⟨
loved deeply for decades, many qualities come to mind. ⟨
most profound to us are these: they have an unquenchable passion for Christ and his church, and they are hopelessly incurable romantics. Both of these qualities are woven into every page of the thirty chapters of this book. Reading it will change your life and your marriage—and quite possibly, your eternity. Therefore, it is absolutely a MUST read!

—Gordon and Theresa Ferguson

————

This is not just a book. This is a gem. Throughout these pages we are invited into all the rooms of the Baird's home, and life. With vulnerability, wisdom, warmth, strength, and deepest love, Al and Gloria share the secrets to their extraordinary marriage. Influencing countless couples around the world through their teaching and example, they don't just share theory, but they share real-life. They not only teach us how to live, but how to grow, and how to die. As I read, I felt overwhelming gratitude, an upward call, warmth, and depth—all through laughter and tears. A must read for every married couple, you will learn to fall deeper in love not only with your spouse, but with your Father in heaven. The Shaws are eternally grateful for this couple's wisdom and beautiful example of a godly marriage.

—Wyndham and Jeanie Shaw

————

Al and Gloria Baird built a great lifelong marriage based on godly wisdom, deep love, and humble hearts, and that is what has laid the foundation for their outstanding book on marriage. They share wise teachings that they learned in the various stages of their life together that will help us address those situations as they come to pass in our married lives as well. Their openness and humility in sharing their many challenging experiences and how they learned to successfully address them will be so very helpful to us all. Thank you, God, for guiding and helping them, and for enabling them to write this book!

—Sam and Geri Laing

Al and Gloria are special friends and, in many ways, family to us. Their lives have inspired us through the years. They have been consistent mentors and inspirations. Their book is a culmination of the many lessons they have taught us. They have done a phenomenal job presenting the challenges of marriage as well as its blessings. This is not just a book on marriage but a lifetime of experiences based on trials, struggles and wonderful moments together. Everything that is written is a beautiful expression and illustration of what God intended for our marriages to be like. Although every marriage is different, this book describes how we go through various stages of marriage. We loved learning how we can be married to a "different" person as we go through the advancing chapters of life from the honeymoon period to widowhood. We have not, personally, gone through all the stages that the Bairds have, but the book has definitely helped us to foresee and to anticipate the road ahead as we to continue to grow and mature in our marriage. We encourage every married couple to read and to study what the Bairds have to say about the basic foundations. It will truly impact you to the very end!

—Frank and Erica Kim

———

Thank you Staci, Kristi and Keri for encouraging your parents to write this wonderful book. We have known Al and Gloria for almost forty years. For most of those years they have been our closest and dearest friends and mentors. The impact they have had on our lives, marriage and family is beyond description. This book, though brief and practical, is rich and deep in the understanding and application of God's principles to build a great marriage. We believe Al and Gloria have had the marriage and life worthy of imitation as described in these pages. We admire their honesty, vulnerability and convictions in sharing the victories and challenges they experienced during their 56 years of marriage. Reading these pages is like hearing their voices once again. This book is truly a beautiful legacy to the love and devotion they have had for the God they have served and for each other, until death separated them...at least for a time.

—John and Nancy Mannel

BUILDING AND GROWING
YOUR MARRIAGE

A
Lifetime
Of

L
O
V
E

Al and Gloria Baird

A Lifetime of Love
Building and Growing Your Marriage
© 2019 by Al Baird and Illumination Publishers

ISBN: 978-1-948450-52-2. Printed in the United States.

Illumination Publishers cares deeply about the environment and uses recycled paper whenever possible.

All Scripture quotations, unless indicated, are taken from the *Holy Bible, New International Version*, (NIV), Copyright © 2011, 2015 by Biblica, Inc. Used by permission. All rights reserved.

Cover design by Roy Appalsamy of Toronto, Canada. Interior layout by Toney Mulhollan. Copy editing by Kiernan Antares.

About the authors: Al and Gloria were both born in Texas. They met, fell in love and married while still in college. After Al finished his PhD in physics from the University of Texas in Austin, they moved to Boston for his first job and to be a part of a church planting. After 15 years in physics research, they decided that Al would give up his physics career and both of them would go into the fulltime ministry as part of a dynamic new church which eventually met in the Boston Garden. They not only helped to shepherd and lead that church, but also served as leaders for planting churches in the Middle East. After 25 years in Boston, they moved to Los Angeles to serve a congregation there. And then 22 years later, in their mid-70s they moved to Phoenix to be near one of their daughters and her family, as well as to work with a church in Phoenix.

LUMINATION PUBLISHERS

www.ipibooks.com
6010 Pinecreek Ridge Court
Spring, Texas 77379-2513

CONTENTS

Introduction 6

C1   Make God the Architect 9

C2   Appreciate Your Differences 14

C3   Be Equal Partners 19

C4   Love One Another 24

C5   Respect Your Mate 30

C6   Be Best Friends 35

C7   Set Right Priorities 40

C8   Communicate 45

C9   Fight Fairly 51

C10   Forgive Everything 56

C11   Always Be Thankful 62

C12   Encourage Each Other 67

C13   Have Realistic Expectations 73

C14   Understand Happiness and Joy 78

C15   Practice Patience 83

C16   Don't Worry 89

C17   Grow Through The Hard Times 93

C18   Enjoy Romance 98

C19   Build Sexual Intimacy 103

C20   Avoid Porn Like the Plague 109

C21   Find Adventure and Make Memories 114

C22   Keep On Dreaming 119

C23   Find a Good Mentoring Couple 124

C24   Handle Your Finances Responsibly 130

C25   Train Your Children 135

C26   Appreciate the Stages of Marriage 140

C27   Enjoy the Empty Nest 145

C28   Share What You Have 150

C29   Recover From Marriage Disaster 155

Epilogue 160

Resources 164

INTRODUCTION

Gloria and I are just eleven months apart in age, so that means for one month each year we have lived the same number of years. When we were both seventy-five, our three daughters, Staci, Kristi, and Keri decided it would be fun to throw us a "150-year-old" birthday party. By that time, we had been married for fifty-five years and had taught hundreds of marriage classes, seminars and conferences all over the world. It was during this party Staci suggested that we write a book on marriage and each of the girls enthusiastically agreed that we needed to leave a marriage legacy for our kids and nine grand children.

At first, Gloria and I were less than excited about the idea. A staggeringly huge number of books have been written about marriage. I read somewhere that in just the last five years, 18,000 new marriage books were written by Christian authors! Why write another one?

But Gloria had been fighting stage four cancer for three years and neither of us was getting any younger. The more we thought, prayed and got advice about the idea we began to get excited because we realized that we could bring a unique perspective to the topic with our wider view than most other authors—from newly wed to grandparents. However, little did we know that before the book was finished, Gloria would pass away. As hard as it has been to cope with losing her and finishing the writing without her, it also adds another dimension to the book that is distinctive: dealing with life after losing a mate.

Not only do half of American marriages die in the divorce court, many more actually die in the heart. Marriage is like a boat in a swift river; you can steer it where you want it to go, or it will drift, usually to places you don't want. And most of the time marriages do drift to dangerous places, not because of bad decisions or actions, but because of neglect and the frantic pace of life.

Gloria and I firmly believe that a marriage has no chance of being all that it can be without a solid commitment to God and an absolute dependence on him. We used to think that it was enough for a committed follower of Jesus to marry another disciple of Jesus (not just Christians in name, but ones who really live it out) to have a good marriage. However, that is only the starting place. As it is said in the scientific world, it is "necessary but not sufficient."

In addition to our individual and collective walk with God, it takes focus and a lot of hard work. But it is well worth it! A romantic and sexual long-term committed relationship is the greatest gift this life can offer. And the beauty is that with God and your efforts, your marriage can be just as great as you both decide for it to be.

This book has 29 chapters including the epilogue, each of which can be read in ten to fifteen minutes. Chapter One starts where the emphasis must be: *on God*. The epilogue ends the book where we will all end at some point: *finishing the race*. May our book help your marriage to become more of what God designed for it to be—a great one.

MAKE GOD THE ARCHITECT

"Unless the LORD builds the house,
the builders labor in vain."
—Psalm 127:1

God is the master architect of all that is, including—the universe and everything in it. He created everything that was, is, or will be. He, the master artist, painted the sunsets that take our breath away, the rainbows that end the storms, the mountains that challenge us to look and climb higher, and the stars that give us a window into the infinite. He breathed life into plants and flowers as well as creatures so small that we cannot see and so large that we keep our distance. He also created us, his ultimate masterpiece, the only part of his creation for which he used himself as the model (Genesis 1:27)! *Therefore, we are special.*

But God was not finished. Just as God is not alone (i.e. The Father, Son, and Holy Spirit), he designed us to thrive in relationships. He gave Adam a mate, Eve—and thus he created humanities' first relationship, which he calls marriage.

GOD'S PURPOSE

Marriage is first and foremost a spiritual relationship. God designed it to work when two people are connected to him individually and as a couple, walking with him every day, obeying Him, and always depending on him in prayer. If we ignore the spiritual dimension, we are ignoring the very God who created marriage, and the only one who can make it work.

Author Gary Thomas, in his book *Sacred Marriage*, puts forth the idea that our relationship in marriage should not be so much about us and our spouse as it is about us and God. He suggests that we use the challenges, joys, struggles, and celebrations of marriage to draw us closer to God. God has designed marriage to help us to be holy first, which will then produce happiness.

We can appreciate that God designed marriage to provide partnership, spiritual intimacy and the ability to pursue Him— together.

SATAN'S LIES

From the beginning of mankind, Satan has done his very best to undermine God's perfect plan. We all pay the price for Adam and Eve allowing Satan to substitute lies for God's truth. And through the ages, in both obvious and subtle ways, the "Father of Lies" continues to corrupt God's marriage design. Consider a few of the lies that Satan currently tells our world, compared to the truth of the matter:

- **Lie #1:** Marriage in today's world is outdated and over-rated. If you love someone, there is no reason to wait for marriage to live together.

Anthropologists Nena and George O'Neill[1] wrote: "Why, in a world of instant and carefree sex, liberalized moral codes and situation ethics, get married at all? Why not just live together?" Besides, if you do decide to get married, it makes more sense to live together first to see if you are compatible. Wouldn't you test drive a car first before you bought it? Today, living together precedes more than half of all first marriages.[2] A major reason couples live together is to learn more about their partner to see if they want to get married.

The Real Truth of the Matter: Statistically, couples who live together before they marry have a separation rate five times that of married couples![3]

- **Lie #2:** Just because someone is married doesn't mean that sex should be confined to that one relationship. Sex and love do not necessarily have to go together.

Open Marriage: A New Life Style for Couples[4] was a best-selling book written in 1972 by Nena and George O'Neill; it was on the New York Times best-seller list for forty weeks and was translated into fourteen languages, selling more than thirty–five million copies. It helped foster the sexual revolution in the 1970s. The O'Neill's conceived open marriage as one in which each partner can develop outside friendships including sex.

The Real Truth of the Matter: Some research shows that the open marriage concept has a 92 percent failure rate.[5]

- Lie #3: Sex is a source of great pleasure; there is no reason to let God control it with his oppressive, controlling, outdated rules of morality. If it feels good, do it.

The Real Truth of the Matter: In the 1970s Redbook Magazine commissioned one of the largest surveys ever conducted on the sexual mores and habits of married women;[6] it surveyed 100,000 women. The results showed that "with notable consistency, the greater the intensity of a woman's religious convictions, the likelier she is to be highly satisfied with the sexual pleasures of marriage." It also found that strictly monogamous women experienced orgasm during sex more than twice as often as promiscuous women. And it found that highly religious women were less likely to engage in sex prior to marriage and more likely to describe their sex lives as "good" or "very good" than moderately—religious or non-religious women. Other studies show that women who marry as virgins have a fifty percent lower divorce rate than the norm.[7]

- Lie #4: Marriage is about finding someone who will be my soul-mate, who will somehow complete me and meet all my needs.

The Real Truth of the Matter: Spiritually speaking, looking for and expecting another human to complete us is a form of idolatry. If we expect our spouse to be 'God' to us, he or she will fail every day. No person can live up to such expectations. My mate is my partner so that we can love each other and spend our lives walking—together down the path that God has laid out for us, as we fulfill his plans for us.

Sadly, marriage has become an institution with an ever-widening back door. In 1886 the divorce rate in the United States was thirty divorces per one thousand marriages; that is only 0.3 percent. One hundred years later, by 1986, the rate had grown almost twenty times to five hundred divorces per one thousand marriages, a fifty percent failure rate.

Over the years, philosophers, social scientists and all manner of self-proclaimed "experts" have tried to address the institution of marriage with recommendations ranging from creative to crazy. The late anthropologist Margaret Mead said, "Modern marriage is archaic in today's context." Her idea was to design marriage in terms of a five-year contract that could be renewed. If a couple chose not to renew their contract, the husband and wife would each go their own way; no divorce would be necessary. Government-financed parents would be provided for any children of the couple who did not renew their contract.

Margaret Mead was divorced three times.[8]

GOD'S PERFECT DESIGN

We once heard an ad on the radio that said, "If you are thinking about building a home and not using an architect, you had better think again." That is also true for building a marriage. God, the master architect, designed marriage with a unique plan which works only if we follow his directions. God's plan for marriage (or his plan for anything else) cannot be improved on. He designed it, he created it, he knows how it will work; our job is to study it and make every effort to follow his blueprint for our marriage. Together, husbands and wives must develop and maintain an absolute dependence on him; that is one of the reasons we put such a strong emphasis in our teaching and counseling on praying together as a couple every day.

The only new car that we ever owned was a 1968 GTO—what a great car! When I (Al) finished my doctorate at the University of Texas and had a real job, that was our first major purchase. We loved that car. Our first job was in Boston; and while we really loved Boston, the long, harsh winters with salt on the roads took their toll on our beautiful car. By the second winter, the rust was showing through. By the fifth year, our beautiful GTO wasn't so beautiful any more.

Like our brand–new GTO, many marriages look shiny and beautiful at the start. But during the cold, harsh storms of life, Satan attacks. The marriages that are not "rust proofed" by following the design of the Master Architect become corroded and ugly.

But here is something amazing about following God's plan

for marriage: if we let him, he can use those storms of life to strengthen our marriages and make them more beautiful. God promises that if we build on him, our marriage will not just survive, but thrive, because *"In all things God works for the good of those who love him..."* (Romans 8:28).

END NOTES

1. Nena O'Neill and George O'Neill, *Open Marriage: A New Life Style for Couples* (M. Evans & Company, 1972), 16.

2. Sheri Stritof, "Essential Cohabitation Facts and Statistics" December 13, 2018, https://www.thespruce.com/cohabitation-facts-and-statistics-2302236.

3. Ibid.

4. Karen Salmansohn, "Do open marriages work?" March 23, 2010, http://www.cnn.com/2010/LIVING/personal/03/23/o.open.marriages.work/.

5. Robert Levin and Ann Levin, "Sexual pleasure: The surprising preferences of 100,000 women" September 1975, Redbook Magazine, 145.

6. Nicholas Wolfinger, "Counterintuitive Trends in the Link Between Premarital Sex and Marital Stability" June 6, 2016, https://ifstudies.org/blog/counterintuitive-trends-in-the-link-between-premarital-sex-and-marital-stability/?utm_source=Media+List&utm_campaign=bd9aa76eb8-sex_divorce_risk_2016_press&utm_medium=email&utm_term=0_a2dbdbdf5e-bd9aa76eb8-109135973.

7. Ana Swanson, "144 years of marriage and divorce in the United States, in one chart" June 23, 2015, https://www.washingtonpost.com/news/wonk/wp/2015/06/23/144-years-of-marriage-and-divorce-in-the-united-states-in-one-chart/?noredirect=on&utm_term=.ef79960d7335.

8. Biography editors, "Margaret Mead" February 27, 2018, https://www.biography.com/people/margaret-mead-9404056.

Chapter Two

APPRECIATE YOUR DIFFERENCES

*"But at the beginning of creation
God 'made them male and female.'"*
—Mark 10:6

We have determined that God is a master architect who must be the designer of our marriage. Yet, no masterful architect uses the same materials and designs in their work but instead uses contrasts in texture, colors, and shapes. God designed us to be different, yet the perfect complement to each other.

What an amazing beginning. God made men and women different from each other. In the beginning of a relationship, our physical differences are a large part of our initial attraction.

As we begin sharing our lives together, we learn that we are VERY different, different in ways that we never imagined. and in many ways that we don't understand. And in some ways that we don't even like. "Why can't a woman be more like a man?" asks Henry Higgins in *My Fair Lady*. Many a husband has asked that question (at least to himself); and just as many frustrated wives have felt the same about their husbands. So begins the marriage adventure.

A very creative and insightful approach to understanding our differences is offered by John Gray in his best seller, *Men Are from Mars, Women Are from Venus*.[1] He has us imagine two different planets, Mars and Venus. On Mars there are only men, and on Venus only women. Using a telescope, the men discovered the beautiful opposite sex on Venus; they built spaceships to reach them and so began some wonderful relationships. Eventually, they migrated together to earth, and over time forgot their roots from Mars and Venus. Then the problems began, because they forgot that their origins were very different.

Almost every married couple has fallen into the common trap of failing to recognize the fundamental differences in the way that God created men and women. Gloria and I certainly did. These differences often divide us, because we don't understand and appreciate them as being a part of his plan to help us be better together. We are equal in the sight of God but that does not mean that we are the same. He created men and women to be different, and one key to a great marriage is working with and appreciating his design rather than being annoyed by it and trying to change it.

Let's consider a few differences. (We should note that the differences we will mention are generalities; there are of course always exceptions.)

THE BRAIN: LOGIC AND EMOTION

A significant difference is often in the way we think, solve problems, and process emotions. The brain structure of men and women is significantly different. The brain has two sides: the left side which is the base of logical thought and the right side which is the base of emotions. Women have four times as many neurons connecting the right and left sides of their brain as do men. The result is that men rely more on their logical left brain to solve a problem one step at a time, and women have more efficient access to both sides of their brain simultaneously, and therefore greater use of their right brain, the emotional side. This brings significant differences in emotional expression and communication in relationships. The female brain is wired to think things through externally using both emotion and logic, and women often process by talking.

The male brain is structured to think things through logically, and men usually find it difficult to process while talking. This wiring difference is most obvious when there is conflict between us. Al often just wants space and time to figure things out when I want a hug and for us to talk things out together. And when I am trying to think through a problem that doesn't involve Al, but am very much wanting his advice, it is not unusual for Al to quickly offer his logical solution, and for me to tell him not to fix it so quickly. Because part of my solution involves my talking it out, I just need for him to listen.

VIEW OF RELATIONSHIP

In general, the appeal of a relationship for a woman IS *the relationship*. Women naturally gravitate towards the idea of marriage and see it as highly appealing. An ideal relationship for her is often one where she feels understood and connected to her man, and her man is often one who truly *understands* her. The ideal relationship for many men is one where they are made to feel like *"the man."* And I, like many men with their wives, don't have the same need for understanding from Gloria, as she does from me. Rather, men in general like to feel respected and appreciated. Men typically enjoy the role of being fixers and givers, so for a man, **the ideal woman** is one who can happily receive. There is nothing sexier or more appealing to him than a happy woman who appreciates everything he has to offer.

GOALS

A man by nature is typically more goal oriented, being strongly motivated by achievement and success. He will see the goal and think through the steps to get there. On the other hand, a woman may have goals, but she often has a deeper interest in people, their feelings, and in building relationships. Men tend to be more preoccupied with practicalities that can be understood through logical deduction, and they are more challenge-and-conquer oriented. This explains their strong interest in sports and their strong desire to win. Consider what happens during many family vacations. He is challenged by the goal of driving four hundred miles a day; while she wants to stop now and then to drink coffee and enjoy the scenery.

COMPETITION, RISK AND SECURITY

Men are competitive; they can make a game out of anything. We were once house sitting for friends, which included watching a twelve-year-old boy. He was a lot of fun, but it was nearly impossible to get him up in time to get ready for school in the morning until finally, I (Al) thought of turning it into a game. Every morning I would time how long it took him from the sounding of the alarm until he was dressed. Each day he would try to set a record and accomplished it with no nagging on my part—I was happy and so was he!

Men are also generally risktakers. They thrill to an adrenalin rush. This is somewhat related to their being goal oriented but is still a different trait. Guys are motivated by anyone daring them to do something that is new or difficult (or even "stupid"!), especially if the challenge comes from or while with a group of friends. The ultimate disgrace is being seen as a coward or "chicken." On the other hand, most women seek security. Because her orientation is inward, toward relationships, nurturing, and "nesting," she puts a premium on safety and security. To a far greater extent than the male, she values qualities like "dependability" and "trustworthiness" in her mate.

HORMONES

Women have several unique and important physical functions, including menstruation, pregnancy and lactation, etc. A woman's hormones are of a different type and more numerous than a man's, and their levels can change dramatically during those events. A man's hormone levels do not change very much; and it is often a shock and adjustment to the husband when he experiences the emotional swings, mood changes, and physical discomfort that can accompany her in such times as her monthly cycle, pregnancy, postpartum, and menopause.

When we were first married Gloria's monthly periods and changes in emotions that accompanied them were a new adjustment for me. I wanted to be sensitive and understanding; so, to anticipate those times I started keeping track of her cycle with a calendar. That was very helpful for both of us, because it prepared me emotionally and enabled me to be extra helpful and encouraging.

DIFFERENCES IN THE BEDROOM

When it comes to physical intimacy, men and women are also very different. In no other area of marriage do our differences create as many opportunities for mutual pleasure or misunderstanding as in the bedroom. A woman's sexual drive tends to be related to her monthly cycle, while a man's drive is fairly constant. Studies show that most women are stimulated more by touch and romantic words, while her husband is stimulated by sight. A man requires little or no preparation for sex, but his wife usually needs significantly more time

A husband needs to know that his wife desires him, and

that results in a sense of well-being that carries over into every other area of his life. Being goal oriented, he not only needs her to meet his physical needs, but he also wants to feel that he can excite her and meet her sexual needs. Understanding these differences and mutually meeting each other's needs is vitally important to a fulfilling marriage.

INSECURITIES

We all have insecurities, but they tend to be gender specific. Wives often wonder things like: Am I attractive to him? Am I loveable? Am I special to him? Would he marry me again? Husbands can struggle with thoughts like: Am I adequate? Does she respect me? Does she admire me? Do I make her happy? Can I satisfy her in the bedroom?

These are just a few of our God-given differences; there are many more. To this list, add our different individual quirks, tastes and personalities. Gloria and I took a significant step forward in our relationship when we began to realize that God purposely made each of us totally unique, and we began to see that together we are better and stronger because of our uniqueness. Each of us has strengths and weaknesses that are specific to the differences that God purposely created between men and women; and when those differences are fitted together into a unified marriage relationship, the result is an incredibly powerful team where each contributes wholeheartedly.

END NOTES _____

1. John Gray, *Men Are from Mars, Women Are from Venus: A Practical Guide for Improving Communication and Getting What You Want in Your Relationships* (HarperCollinsPublishers, 1992).

Chapter 3

BE EQUAL PARTNERS

*As the Scriptures say, "A man leaves
his father and mother and is joined
to his wife, and the two are
united into one."*
—Ephesians 5:31

This chapter is adapted from a chapter that I (Gloria) wrote in a book coauthored with Kay McKean.[1]

Since men and women have many differences, how can they function as one? If one is from Mars and the other from Venus, how can they use their differences productively?

Marriages come in all different shapes and sizes. With each husband and wife there is a unique set of backgrounds, personalities, strengths and weaknesses. So many variables compose a complete person that the meshing of two lives into one is quite an adventure. In fact, it is nothing short of a miracle, when those two lives are really unified in a vibrant, growing and fulfilling relationship. God's plan is amazing, and only as we follow that plan will our marriages be truly successful. From the beginning God saw that it was not good for man to be alone, so God made a helper suitable for him (Genesis 2:18). By God's design he made woman from man's rib—from his side (Genesis 2:22). The very first marriage was husband and wife, side by side, adult to adult.

In today's world most marriages have veered far off the track of God's design. Many times, our role models are anything but godly. We've seen the overpowering husband and father who has everyone cowering before him. We've seen the matriarch; the wife and mother "ruling the roost" and calling the shots. And we've seen everything in between. Without even realizing it, we imitate the examples around us, whether good or bad. It is helpful to step back and try to take an objective look at the interactions in our marriages.

An interesting theory of personality and interpersonal relationships known as *Transactional Analysis* was developed by psychologist Eric Berne.[2] According to his theory we function and interact with each other in any of three different ways: Parent to Child, Child to Parent or Adult to Adult. A relationship between two adults will be unhealthy if one functions as the parent and the other as the child. Only when we relate as adult to adult will our interactions be fulfilling. It is faith-building to remember that God's plan from the beginning was that we, as husband and wife, function side by side, adult to adult.

YOU ARE NOT YOUR HUSBAND'S MOTHER

The mothering instinct is strong in us women. It is God's plan for a mother with her child, but not for a wife with her husband. You may be saying, "Well, my husband acts like a child, so that's why I treat him the way I do." Whatever the logic, it looks bad, sounds bad, and is bad! It is not God's design.

Al still teases me about one of our first bumps as newlyweds moving into our apartment. He was unpacking dishes and putting them into the kitchen cabinet. In some not-so-subtle ways I let him know the kitchen was my domain, and I would decide where to put things. We can laugh about it now, but it wasn't very funny then. Al has never wanted to take over the kitchen, but it would have been a smoother move if I had been humble. We can be very "picky" about minor things.

I have a vivid memory of being in a group when I corrected some small detail of something Al was saying. The other men in the group immediately reacted by rolling their eyes and making faces. I was defenseless, and I remember the pain of the moment. Our criticalness and "mothering" often turn into a bossy and even nagging tone as we work hard to get our point across. We need to be reminded of Solomon's words: *"a quarrelsome wife is like a constant dripping"* (Proverbs 19:13). Not exactly an endearing description!

YOU ARE NOT YOUR HUSBAND'S CHILD

In some marriages the interactions may have the wife in the child role. The husband may be very controlling or demanding; the wife may be trying to keep the peace or avoiding taking responsibility. Patterns start early in marriage with each of us bringing our own background and "baggage" into the mix. Typically, the dynamics in our family background get carried into our marriage. A wife's immaturity or irresponsibility may elicit a strong parental response from her husband. Some husbands are so controlling that they intimidate their wives into a childlike cowering or silence.

In one marriage Al and I counseled, the husband was so overbearing that his wife developed a response of talking like a child; the tone of her voice totally changed in conversations with him. He used his anger and putdowns to manipulate his wife into "submission." His continual criticism of even small household chores eroded his wife's confidence. More commonly and less extreme, I've heard women say that their husband made them feel like a child by reminding them over and over to make a phone call or pay a bill.

YOU ARE AN ADULT

We may use the term "grownup" for adult, but even we "older" husbands and wives are still growing. Recently, I have grown in my conviction to love the truth. In several group settings it has been eye opening to observe dynamics and patterns between husbands and wives. Consciously and unconsciously some develop ways of silencing one another to avoid painful or embarrassing exposure of our weaknesses.

One husband described the condition of their relationship by saying, "We're doing good, aren't we?" The wife agreed, but later told the truth when she was in a "safe place" and would be heard. We certainly all need a safe environment where we can express our deepest hurts and fears, but we cannot bypass the truth while waiting for the perfect opportunity.

Another wife began to express some ways her husband had hurt her, only to glance at him and immediately minimize what she had just said with, "But you have changed a lot." By being silent, minimizing, or agreeing outwardly while inwardly disagreeing we are really being dishonest. We need to love the truth more than we even love the relationship with each other. Our love for the truth needs to motivate and propel us to speak the truth in love (Ephesians 4:15). For we who stuff our feelings and hide the truth, we need to have the courage to get the facts of our marriages out in the open.

Recently I heard of a woman who said, "I want to mean what I say and say what I mean...and not be mean!" That's the spirit we should go for. We need to be grateful for the people God has put in our lives who can disciple and help us to speak the truth and to speak it in love. Most of all we need to not be afraid of the truth and remember *"the truth will set you free."* (John 8:32)

Being an adult has a lot to do with accepting responsibility. In most of the appointments that Al and I have with married couples we try to help each person see and accept responsibility for his or her actions. Somehow marriage partners often want to shift the blame saying, "If he wouldn't _____, then I wouldn't _____." Certainly, we are connected, and we do affect each other. On the other hand, it is vital to recognize that I am the only one that I can control and change.

Al and I had a exchange that showed me I still have some growing to do in this area. We were getting ready to go on a date; Al was on the phone, and I needed to know when we were going to leave. We have agreed not to interrupt each other when one of us is on the phone. All I wanted was a quick hand signal from Al, but what I got was a glare as he mouthed, "I'm on the phone!" I retreated, feeling aggravated and hurt. As soon as he got off the phone, he came in and apologized and reminded me of our agreement. That should have taken care of it all, but I held on to my feelings. I let Al's response control my mood rather than maturely accepting my responsibility for breaking our agreement. Fortunately, I came to my senses and repented before I spoiled the whole evening. As I looked at my reaction, I realized that too often I connect to someone else's action when I should disconnect and be responsible for my own action.

YOU ARE ON HIS TEAM

God planned for the wife to be a helper "suitable" for the husband. It was God's intent for husband and wife to be together—we need each other. We make a great team, when we work together. But usually couples are very different. One husband told us about seeing their differences clearly on their honeymoon. They went mountain climbing. He was determined to get to the top no matter what; she wanted to have fun all along the way. If it had been up to the wife, they would never have reached the top. If it had been up to the husband, they would have had no fun. As a team they were able to have fun reaching the top.

In our marriages, we have different strengths and weaknesses. It is amazing to see the incredible way God works to blend us together to be a team. We can also feel the destructive pulls from Satan to use our differences to divide us. It is up to us individually to appreciate each other and to determine to do our part to work together. Part of the beauty of marriage is seeing how much better and more effective we are as a team than by ourselves. And our team is one of two adults, being honest with each other and with those in our lives. The marriage team works with honesty but without love our honesty will feel more like a business arrangement.

END NOTES _____

1. Gloria Baird and Kay McKean, *Love Your Husband* (Discipleship Publications International, 2001), 43. Available from www.ipibooks.com.

2. Eric Berne, *Games People Play: The Psychology of Human Relationship* (Grove Press, 1964).

Chapter 4

LOVE ONE ANOTHER

"Let him lead me to the banquet hall,
and let his banner over me be love."
—Song of Songs 2:4

Now that we have defined marriage as a team who appreciates differences and speaks honestly, we must learn to love well. Love is one of the most powerful and intense emotions that we as humans experience. John Paul Getty, once the richest man on earth, who was married five times, said, "I'd give my entire fortune for one person to truly love me."

Poets and song writers have written about it ever since the birth of language. Songs like *I Wanna Love You Forever* sung by Jessica Simpson:[1]

"I wanna love you forever
And this is all I'm asking of you
10,000 lifetimes together
Is that so much for you to do..."

Beautiful, heart moving verses often come from the unlikeliest of people. Bruce Lee, the late martial arts expert, who is best known for destroying the bad guys waxed eloquently "Love is like a friendship caught on fire. In the beginning a flame, very pretty, often hot and fierce, but still only light and flickering. As love grows older, our hearts mature and our love becomes as coals, deep, burning and unquenchable."

But what is love? The word is used in many ways. I love my mate. I love my kids. I love my life. I love my dog. I love my car. I love sex. I love steak. I love football. I love a particular movie or TV show. In English we have one word for all the different varieties of love. In the Persian language there are seventy-six different words that are translated as "love!" Since our principal guide and authority for this book is the Bible let's consider the language in which most of the New Testament was written; Greek. In the Greek there are eight words that are translated as love. We will examine those words shortly, but first we need to address a very important question.

Is love in marriage a feeling or an action? Some will argue that true love, the kind of love that keeps a couple together for a lifetime, is not a feeling. It is said that one of the great tragedies of Western culture is that we have equated love with warm, emotional feelings. "If it is a feeling, what if I'm not feeling it?" They say that this is why love can be commanded, as in Ephesians 5:25: "*Husbands, love your wives*"; and love can be taught and learned, as in Titus 2:4, where the older women are instructed to teach the younger women to love their husbands. God doesn't command emotions, but he often commands attitudes and behavior; and whatever God commands, he enables us to do.

Others will argue that marital love should not be simply the result of obeying a command or deciding to be in love. They say that a meaningful relationship is filled with and driven by strong romantic feelings. We marry as a result of 'feeling love' or 'falling in love', and the experience of 'falling in love' involves intense emotional, usually passionate feelings for our future mate.

We believe the correct answer lies in the combination of the essence of these two arguments and that our marriage will not reach the heights that God intends if we lean too far to either side. We contend that a God inspired marriage will incorporate seven of the eight Greek words that we refer to that are translated as "love" in English, and these words carry with them a mixture of feelings and actions. (We will exclude the eighth one, *mania*, because it is an obsessive love based on selfishness, and not something we want in our marriage.) Let's look at these definitions and see how they apply to love in marriage. (We are certainly not Greek scholars, but we do know how to use a Greek lexicon.)

Philautia: (Love of self) Jesus said the second greatest command is to love others as we love ourselves (Mark 12:31). Love of self involves the challenge of realizing that we are nothing without God, but that by his grace we are his children with all its privileges. Low self-esteem and a feeling of worthlessness are not a good foundation for a solid marriage, but neither is superiority and entitlement. A spirit of gratitude and humility is a good starting place.

Storge: (Familial love) This is love that results from being in the same family. It is an attachment love; when you feel attached to someone, you will care for their well-being. It grows out of having similar interests or experiences rather relying on passion. This is the natural affection between mates; you like each other, and you enjoy being together because you belong to each other.

Ludus: (Playful love) This describes couples who want to have fun with each other in their relationship. It often involves the playful affection between lovers with the flirting and teasing that often accompanies it. The couples who practice *ludus* make sure to take time to enjoy one other.

Eros: (Erotic love) This love involves sexual passion and desire. It is a highly sensual and intense style of love that values enjoying sexual pleasure together (See the chapter on sexual intimacy).

Pragma: (Lasting love) This is a love that ages, matures and develops well over the years and will stand the test of time. Pragmatic lovers want to meet their mate's needs and are confident that their partner will do the same for them. This style of love, as much as any of the seven, is at work in cultures where arranged marriages are common.

Philia: (Affectionate love) This love usually depends on a deep friendship (See the chapter on friendship) that has been forged by being together for a long time and perhaps enduring many hardships together. In relationships with philia, affection and support characterize the relationship. This type of love is extremely important in marriage; you should be each other's best friends and treat each other as equal partners. When you're not just their spouse but also their friend you feel a great affection for each other and support each other in struggles and decisions.

Agape: (Selfless love) This is the highest, purest and most radical type of love and is the noblest word for love in the Greek language. It is the word used to describe God, when it is said that *"God is love"* (1 John 4:8). It is also the love that we are called to have for each other as husband and wife, based on an unbreakable commitment and an unconditional, undying, and selfless love that has no limits on giving. It is the stuff that holds a marriage together through all kinds of storms. Agapic lovers view their mates as blessings and wish to take care of them. They get more pleasure from giving in the relationship than from receiving. Agape requires one to be forgiving, patient, understanding, loyal, and willing to make sacrifices for their partner.

When we were just beginning to date, Gloria and I were apart for two summers, long before email, cell phones, and texting existed. So, we wrote each other almost daily. It was really exciting to recently go back and reread those letters from almost sixty years ago. (Yes, we still have them all.) What was interesting was to see the progression of our love; it was clear from the way we signed our letters. Early on, we were very tentative and insecure, not wanting to sound farther along with our feelings than the other was. We began by signing our letters –"Love." Then one of us dared to sign it, "Love ya," eagerly waiting to see if the other signed it the same way. Next, one of us ventured, "Love you." Oh, happy day! Then came the exciting day of "I love you." After we were married, it grew from there to "I love you to infinity!"

Husbands are given a very specific charge to love their wives in Ephesians 5:25–28: *"Husbands, love your wives, just as Christ loved the church and gave himself up for her...husbands ought to love their wives as their own bodies. He who loves his wife loves himself."* In the same passage wives are called to respect their husbands, and we will discuss that in the following chapter; but it appears that God created our wives with the need to receive an extra-large amount of love from their husbands.

Gary and Barbara Rosenberg, in their book *The Five Love Needs of Men and Women,*[2] surveyed seven hundred couples and found five main ways that men and women need to be shown love by their mates. In keeping with Ephesians 5, we focus here on their findings for the needs of the women:

1. **Unconditional love and acceptance (Agape)**—She wants to feel treasured, important, special and unique.

2. **Emotional intimacy and great communication**—She wants to be heard and understood, and to understand her husband. She wants a marriage that has vulnerable sharing of inner thoughts, feelings, spirit and true self.

3. **Spiritual intimacy**—She wants God to be inextricably woven throughout the marriage relationship. She needs to be growing spiritually and watching her husband grow spiritually and leading the home.

4. **Encouragement and affirmation**—Encourage her by understanding her wiring, giving her first place, pointing out her potential, and appreciating her contribution.

5. **Companionship**—It is all about togetherness. She needs her husband to work hard at the marriage; to laugh together, play together, stay the course, and work out the inevitable differences between you.

While the above list came from a survey focusing on a woman's need for love, both men and women need love. This list could also describe most men's need for love. Love is the greatest way that we imitate God since God is love.

Most of us used to dream about finding that one special love, who would fulfill all our needs and desires—who was always affectionate, friendly, playful, erotic, selfless, and stable. In reality, no person can satisfy all of those things, and neither can you or I. While we won't have a perfect marriage, we can still have one in which both of us are trying to grow in each of those seven meanings of love taken from the Greek.

No, your heart may not skip a beat every time you see your beloved after twenty-five years of marriage and a few kids, but hopefully it will still flutter often. And, you will treasure the partner who accompanies you in a lifetime of shared love, a lifetime of struggling and working and growing together. You will feel and experience going through life with and being loved by your partner; someone who admired you when you were young, middle aged, and old, and they will feel the same about you. That is what Gloria and I have experienced, and we can only hope and pray that for each of you.

END NOTES _____

1. *I Wanna Love You Forever*, written by Louis Biancaniello and Sam Watters.

2. Gary Rosberg and Barbara Rosberg, *The 5 Love Needs of Men and Women* (Tyndale Momentum, 2017).

Chapter 5

RESPECT YOUR MATE

"Show proper respect to everyone..."
—1 Peter 2:17

We all want to feel loved, and one of the best ways to show love is to show respect for each other. This chapter is written more from a husband's perspective about respect.

Otis Redding, one of the great rhythm-and-blues singers and songwriters wrote the hit song "RESPECT", in which he described a man's need for respect from his woman. Two years later, Aretha Franklin, often called the Queen of Soul, rewrote and sang the song from a woman's perspective; and according to *Rolling Stone*, it became the fifth biggest hit of all time.[1] Both versions connected emotionally with the listening audience. Both versions correctly recognize that respect is necessary for any relationship to be successful. Mutual respect is one of the basic ingredients of any meaningful partnership, and the lack of it can destroy a marriage, or at least, lead to a painful, stressful, and unhappy life for a couple.

What is "respect?" How do we define it? A dictionary definition states that respect is "a feeling of deep admiration for someone elicited by their abilities, qualities, or achievements." But "respect" is a word like "love", "empathy," or "compassion;" everyone agrees it is a desirable quality, but there are countless ideas about their meanings. Respect is difficult to define because it can mean different things to different people, and more specifically, can mean different things to men than to women. Both have the need for respect, but if we don't understand how the other one defines it, how can we satisfy each other? It is like throwing a dart at a board without knowing the location of the bull's eye.

God created us in such a way that while we are very different, men and women need both love and respect, but at differing levels and in different ways. The Apostle Paul gives very practical instructions for a Godly marriage in Ephesians 5:21-33. Verse 33 reads, *"However, each one of you must love his wife as he loves himself, and the wife must respect her husband."* The implication here is that, though every person needs both love and respect, God gave men a special, deep need for respect, and he gave women the same deep need for love. It is hard for most women to understand or even imagine that men want respect more than love. While it doesn't mean he doesn't value or want or need love, he needs respect to fill his tank.

A landmark book on this subject is *Love & Respect* by Dr. Emerson Eggerichs.[2] Eggerichs sites the results of two studies that affirm the typical man's need for respect over love. In one national study, four hundred men were given a choice: If forced to choose one of the following, which would they prefer to endure?: a) to be left alone and unloved in the world or b) to feel inadequate and disrespected by everyone. Seventy-four percent of these men said they would prefer being alone and unloved in the world; they chose respect!

In another national survey on male-female relationships that started with the premise that conflict is a natural, day-to-day part of life, seven thousand people were asked if in the middle of conflict with their mates, they would be likely to feel a) my mate doesn't respect me right now or b) my mate doesn't love me right now." Eighty-three percent of the men chose a) my mate doesn't respect me right now, while seventy-two percent of the women chose b) my mate doesn't love me right now.

Eggerichs defines what he calls the "Crazy Cycle." The wife primarily needs love, and the husband primarily needs respect. Without love from him, she reacts without respect; without respect from her, he reacts without love. Around and around it goes. This is the Crazy Cycle. The cycle can be broken by either one giving the other what they need. How the need for love and the need for respect play off one another has everything to do with the kind of marriage you will have.

Clearly, since love and respect are commanded (Ephesians 5:33), it follows that they are to be unconditional. Yes, this means that wives are to respect their husbands UNCONDITIONALLY, just as men are to love their wives unconditionally. (This in no way excuses a husband for not being worthy of respect or for not loving his wife unconditionally.) In the marriage relationship, respect is not earned, but rather it is given, just as love is. A husband is called to love a disrespectful wife, and a wife is called to respect an unloving husband. This is one of the keys to a fulfilling and glorious marriage, but it is only possible with the faith and confidence that God is working to make up the difference and is helping us grow and change. Once again, let us emphasize that this kind of marriage that God intends is possible only with him working daily at the center of the relationship, overcoming our own shortcomings.

Husbands at some level feel insecure and inadequate and need affirmation from our wives. Wives must understand we men aren't half as big and strong and impervious to being hurt as we may seem or pretend to be. One of our greatest fears is not being good enough as a husband and father. To feel like we are not measuring up in the marriage is seriously debilitating; but feeling the belief in us from our mate is incredibly motivational. This need is described in Kenny Rogers' song, *She Believes in Me*.[3] One verse says,

> *"And she believes in me,*
> *I'll never know just what she sees in me*
> *I told her someday if she was my girl, I could change the world*
> *With my little songs, I was wrong*
> *But she has faith in me, and so I go on trying faithfully*
> *And who knows maybe on some special night, if my song is right*
> *I will find a way, find a way"*

Here are some common things that most men need to feel respect from you wives:

1. Tell us what you appreciate, admire, and respect about us (Yes, using the word "respect" can mean a lot). We want to know that you are proud of us and specifically "why". Telling us "face to face" is great, but so is writing a card or a text. Doing this daily is a habit that will

pay huge dividends, because it is both tremendously encouraging, and will help you to think positively.

2. Tell others, especially the kids, what you respect about us. To hear from someone else that you have been bragging about us lets us know that you are proud of us.

3. Accept that you married a less-than-perfect partner, just as you are. Remember that we are all a work in progress. Patience, please.

4. Do not nag. Find ways to motivate us that are helpful rather than frustrating and repetitive. Remember the admonition from Proverbs 21:19, *"Better to live in a desert than with a quarrelsome and nagging wife."* Use a loving tone.

5. Appreciate our desire to please God and to lead our family to follow Him.

6. And finally, one of the most important areas of all: appreciate us sexually. Probably in no other area are we so insecure and vulnerable. The sexual relationship is very important to us. We discuss this in more detail in the chapter on sexual intimacy. Not only do we need sexual release, but we need to know that we please you sexually. We very much want you to need us sexually. We are insecure about our size, our performance, your desire for us and many other things in the bedroom. Your respect for us sexually is hugely important to our security.

On July 14, 2018, I lost Gloria to cancer after a six-year battle. It was the best fifty-six years that I could have ever imagined, beyond my wildest dreams. We had many great plans in 2018 and had no idea the end would come so soon. I want to share what she wrote on her last Valentine's Day card to me, with no idea the end was so near. I share this as an example of how a wife can respect her man and totally fill him up. This card is now one of my greatest possessions.

> More than ever I appreciate, love, admire and treasure the man you are—the man God gave me!! We would never have dreamed all the ADVENTURES—exciting ones and challenging ones God has and is taking us on!! It's still hard to believe that we can love each other MORE & MORE as the days and years go by. I can't be thankful enough for how much you love me, serve me, give to me and support me through all the ups and downs. You are my man—worthy of all my RESPECT and admiration. Thanks for letting God mold and shape and fill you.
>
> I'm forever yours. —GB"

Let's be eager to show respect. Respect for each other builds safety in our interactions which makes true friendship possible.

END NOTES

1. It was rated #5 in The 500 Greatest Songs of All Time, *Rolling Stone Magazine,* December 2004, Issue 963.

2. Emerson Eggerichs, *Love & Respect: The Love She Most Desires; The Respect He Desperately Needs* (Integrity Publishers, 2004).

3. *She Believes in Me,* written by Steve Gibb and song by Kenny Rogers, 1979. It reached No. 1 in the Billboard Country Music Charts.

Chapter 6

BE BEST FRIENDS

"Happy is the man who finds a true friend, and far happier is he who finds hat true friend is his wife."
—Franz Schubert,
18th century composer

In 1960, singer Jackie Wilson's song *A Woman, A Lover, A Friend*[1] was a number one hit. The first verse said:

*"I want somebody to hold my hand
Somebody to love me and understand
I want a woman
I want a lover
I want a friend."*

Many of us guys would say "amen" to this song, and this would be the order we would choose: lover and then friend. However, research has shown the order is wrong. Friedrich Nietzsche, 19th century philosopher said: "It is not a lack of love, but a lack of friendship that makes unhappy marriages." Recent studies confirm the absolute value of friendship. According to a study conducted by the National Bureau of Economic Research in Canada,[2] those who claimed their spouse was their best friend had the highest level of happiness. They had double the happiness rate compared to couples who didn't say their spouse was their best friend.

Marriage guru John Gottman,[3] professor at the University of Washington and perhaps one of the most respected researchers of marriage over the last twenty-five years, says that his research clearly indicates that "happy marriages are based on a deep friendship." In fact, he finds that the emotional connection that married couples share is five times more important than their physical intimacy. That doesn't mean that physical intimacy or romance is not important in the marriage. Rather, Gottman found that the quality of a married couple's friendship is the most important predictor of satisfaction with sex, romance, and passion; couples who are good friends are usually more sexually satisfied. All of this makes sense.

The percent of time that any of us spend in the physical act of making love is really small compared to the total amount of time we spend together overall. Now don't get us wrong, that small percent of time can be the top-of-the-mountain experience or the icing on the cake—and we love icing! But don't forget the rest of the cake; the other time we spend together as a couple. If we value, enjoy and treasure all that time, it makes our bedroom experience all that much better. As we heard someone say, "All of the time out of the bedroom is really just foreplay!"

Solomon, inspired by God in the Bible's marriage manual, wrote: *"This is my beloved, and this is my friend"* (Song of Songs 5:16). Jeremy Taylor, a famous author of the 17th century wrote "True love is friendship set on fire." Great marriages all revolve around the foundation of friendship. But strangely, not much has been written about friendship in marriage. You'll find countless volumes on romance, intimacy and passion in marriage, but not as much exclusively about how to be friends as husbands and wives. In fact, we recently browsed the table of contents and indexes of the dozens of books on marriage in our library and found very few that even included the word "friend" or "friendship."

"Friend" is defined in various dictionaries as "a person who you like and enjoy being with, a person who knows you, who likes and trusts you, a favored companion, one who supports and sympathizes with you." We suggest that you can have a great discussion if you as a couple sit down and discuss what a good friendship means to you, and which characteristics are most important to you.

How partners define "friend" is somewhat different for each of us. The word "friendship" conjures up thoughts of honesty, vulnerability, companionship, and mutual respect. Your mate should be the person you value the most, meaning they are the one you consult with first, depend on most and whose well-being you think about before your own.

For the remainder of this chapter, we are going to focus on just a few practical aspects of best friendship in marriage. We will expand on each of these areas (and more) in other chapters of this book.

HAVE FUN TOGETHER

When you are best friends, not only are you okay doing nothing together, but you'd rather do nothing with your mate than do something with anyone else. You can just be yourself and let your guard down. Common marriage vows say, "For better or for worse," and life is going to give you your share of both. Don't be overly serious. Whenever things get rough find something to laugh about; laugh a lot together. Like most couples, Gloria and I have divergent tastes and preferences about many things. I love sports; she, not so much. She loves romance novels and movies which are not on my list of favorite things. Our friendship causes us to do things together that we probably would not do separately. When she wants to see the latest chick flick, I will go with her and enjoy it because she enjoys it. When my favorite football team is playing on TV, she will sit with me and cheer just as loudly as I do. That's what best friends do.

BE HONEST WITH EACH OTHER

Friendship helps us feel safe enough to be open with one another without worrying about being judged or feeling insecure. You can tell each other everything; in fact, you often can't wait to talk to each other. You hold each other accountable, willing to speak the truth to each other, always forgiving but not excusing. Friendship is not always sweet and warm. There must be room for confrontation. Since our partner is our best friend there are things that we share that are so intimate and private that we will not tell anyone else. Spouses as best friends have shown themselves to be trustworthy and can handle our imperfections. We feel safe and challenged to become whom we really can be. The best of friends will not only comfort us if we are agitated, but they will agitate us if we get too comfortable.

GET TIME ALONE, TOGETHER

We all work hard to keep up with schedules, work, finances, church activities, and taking care of the home, so we must put a priority on "just us" time. Friendship must be nurtured regularly or it can become just a business relationship. We have seen too many couples become distant and business-like in their marriage where careers have developed and children have come into the picture then the priority of emotional connection has been left to die on the vine. A good first step is to find activities that you like to do together and make the time do them. Regularly take a night or weekend away alone together. Have regularly scheduled dates so you can spend time giving your undivided attention to each another.

BELIEVE IN EACH OTHER

An African proverb that states: "A friend is someone who knows your song and sings it to you when you have forgotten it." Those who love you are not fooled by mistakes you have made or negative images you have of yourself. They remember your beauty when you feel ugly, your wholeness when you are broken, your innocence when you feel guilty, and your purpose when you are confused. We feel that our partner is our ally, has our back, and would not take advantage of our vulnerability. They are there for us in our time of need.

Our partner supports us to become who we can be, so our potential is maximized through our partner's belief in us. With his or her emotional support, we can take risks, try new things, and face our fears because our friend is there to catch us if we fall. I'm Gloria's biggest fan, and she is mine. If you were in our home every day, you would observe that the words we say to each other are overwhelmingly positive. Why? Because, if we're going to be best friends, we're going to continually do and say things that assure our mate that we believe in him or her. We're going to do the things that draw us to one another and open us up to each another.

COMMUNICATE AFFECTION

Since friendship involves so many strong, positive characteristics, the importance and value of expressing them to each other shouldn't be surprising. The Bible stresses this in many places. I know that Gloria loves me and appreciates me, but I need for her to express it often, and vice versa. Many times and in many ways; with words, looks or actions we communicate love and affection every day.

Gottman has found that the principles that make a marriage work are "surprisingly simple." Happily married couples aren't smarter or more beautiful than others, and they don't live in castles in the clouds where there are no conflict or negative feelings. They've simply learned to let their positive feelings about each other and communication of them override their negative ones. They express their love not just in big ways but through small gestures day in and day out. They do little things every day to stay connected and to show each other they care.

Negative sentiment is powerful and destructive to marriage. Gottman's research[3] shows that to build a happy marriage, couples routinely need eight to twenty positive interactions for every negative one! This means our positive thoughts about each other and our marriage are so dominant that they can drown out and overwhelm the negative ones, so that we feel optimistic about each other.

In our more than five decades together, we have experienced life's peaks and valleys together. For us the word "together" makes all the difference. Together the highs have been higher and the lows have not been so low. All because we are best friends.

END NOTES _____

1. *A Woman, A Lover, A Friend,* was written by Sid Wyche and song by Jackie Wilson, 1960. It reached No. 1 on the R&B Music Charts.

2. John F. Helliwell and Shawn Grover, "How's Life at Home? New Evidence on Marriage and the Set Point for Happiness" December 2014, NBER Working Paper No. 20794, https://www.nber.org/papers/w20794.

3. John Gottman, *The Seven Principles For Making Marriage Work* (Harmony Books, 2015).

Chapter 7

SET RIGHT PRIORITIES

"That is why a man leaves his father
and mother and is united to his wife,
and they become one flesh."
—Genesis 2:24

Best friends who are married need to set priorities to keep the friendship growing. In today's world it seems like we are constantly busy, with more that we need to do than we can possibly get done. The demands of life are waiting for us to get out of bed every morning. Emails and texts sent throughout the night come streaming in at the simple touch of a button. Kids need to get ready for school, lunches need to be made, and rides and activities must be arranged. From the very start of the morning we can quickly begin to feel as though everything around us is spinning, and there is no way to slow it down. Most of us have demanding jobs and long commutes, and our work is not done when we come home. After a long day at work we still must prepare dinner, take care of the house, raise our kids, and try to get at least a little couple time together.

But, each of us have been given the same 24 hours in a day. It doesn't matter who we are, how influential we are, whether we're rich or poor, young or old. We all have the same amount of time. Our life will be shaped by how we choose to spend that time, and that's why we must make choices. Prioritizing is an essential part of life—whether or not we realize that we're doing it. Every minute of every day, we're ranking and giving priority to the various things we need or want to do and making decisions based on the importance we give to each option. Priorities are and will continue to be one of the biggest issues in every marriage. When our priorities are out of whack, our marriages will suffer. And when they're set correctly, things go much better. If your marriage isn't high on your list of priorities, you can't expect it to thrive!

GOD MUST COME FIRST

If we are really disciples of Jesus, we are going to make God and his will our top priority. Since we believe that the creator of the universe loves us enough to sacrifice Jesus for us, and that he created us to have an eternal relationship with him, how could we make any choice other than living for him and seeking his will as our number one priority in life? Martin Luther said, "Preach and live as though Jesus Christ had been crucified yesterday, had risen this morning and was coming again tomorrow." Sadly, that is not the choice for most people. Most go through life not having a clue as to what life is about. Freddie Mercury, lead vocalist of the rock group Queen, just weeks before he died of AIDS sang his huge hit song, "The Show Must Go On" which contains the haunting lyric, "...does anybody know what we are living for?"[1] So many people have that same question, with no answers.

NEXT COMES YOUR MARRIAGE

When God created marriage, he gave his expectation for relationships between husband and wife: *"That is why a man leaves his father and mother and is united to his wife, and they become one flesh."* (Genesis 2:24). Marriage was the very first relationship that God created, and he expects it to have the number one priority among all our relationships, other than our relationship with him. With his design, every marriage can succeed; and it's not very complicated. It's all about priorities. When the Bible says we leave our father and mother, it's really saying that we reprioritize our lives. The moment we marry, our spouse becomes our top human priority.

It comes down to a very basic concept: if you're making your marriage a priority every day, the level of stability and satisfaction you achieve will influence all other areas in your life. Many people believe that the kids should always come first; but if your relationship with your spouse isn't in great shape, your parenting and many other things will suffer as well. This is why problems often develop when children enter the picture;

priorities get out of whack. At that point, husband and wife often pour their energy into the children or work to advance their careers. Then, the top priority of making their marriage relationship great is lost. The husband and wife stop focusing the needed attention on each other.

The same is true for our jobs and our relationships with friends and family—our marriage should be the closest human relationship we have. Our mate is the person we share our life with, and its quality is going to affect how we interact with the rest of the world. If we're upset about an unresolved argument, discouraged because we feel disunified, frustrated about a problematic sex life, and so on, we'll take these problems with us to work.

Marital stress will influence how we interact with the kids, and it will affect the quality of time spent with friends and family. However, when we are making our marriage the top priority, the good feelings will also spill over into these other arenas. We will be more positive and more energetic. we will feel more connected to our whole family, we will be less distracted at work, and our interactions with friends and family will be all the more enjoyable because we are happy and truly connected with each other. A strong marriage has a major impact on our entire life.

With the proper priority on marriage, there are also many things to prioritize within the marriage itself; time spent together, minimizing conflict, our sex life, and so on. Only we can know the specific areas of our marriage that need the most work, but like anything else, we must spend time in prayer and make the effort together if we want things to continually change for the better. Whatever needs improvement, put it front and center and continually focus on doing everything you can to make your marriage the best it's ever been.

HOW TO DO IT

It is one thing to conceptualize the need for priorities, but how do we take the concepts from these pages and incorporate them into our lives? Here are a few practical applications that we have found helpful in setting the right priorities:

1. A guiding question is always, "What would Jesus do?" (1 John 2:6)

2. Work out the specifics of implementing the priorities with your spouse. You might start with a question like this: "I want us to make our marriage a priority every day. How can we do that?" What you think it takes to make your mate a top priority could be completely different than how they see it. Remember, you and your spouse are constantly changing and evolving, so questions like this keep you in touch with each other's current thinking.

3. Work at living out the priorities every day. Pray together every day. Encourage each other every day in some specific way. Look each other in the eye and tell them you love them every day. Kiss like you mean it every day.

4. Dream about the future. Imagine yourselves as healthy sixty-five-year-olds. What do you hope to see? Plan for that to become reality.

5. Schedule regular alone time together. It may be a regularly scheduled date night, love-making time, a weekend away together, etc. Once it is on the calendar, make it a priority.

6. Find a like-minded couple who will help you keep your priorities. (See chapter on mentors). You can help each other work towards your goals together. With so much going on in life, we can easily lose focus. These friends can encourage you to live your life in line with your stated priorities.

7. Prioritize time with your mate over extended family members and friends. Expectations of relatives and friends can become over-bearing. Find the proper balance. Al always makes me feel like he would rather be with me than anyone else. Because he makes me feel that way, I feel good about him spending a reasonable amount of time with his friends.

8. Prioritize your mate over your time on social media and the Internet. Today, it's very easy to spend hours on social media entertaining yourself but be careful about how much time you spend surfing the web. Set limits so you can preserve your time together.

9. Gloria and I continually monitor and evaluate the amount of time we spend on social media, the Internet and television. For many years we resisted having a television in our bedroom, because it didn't help either our love life or sleep. In the last few years we did yield to the television in the bedroom temptation, but under very tight and mutually agreed on controls. We still advise younger married couples to resist.

God, through our marriage, has given us an incredible way to enjoy life. But the enjoyment doesn't come from doing monumental things occasionally. It happens when we do the little things that matter most each day, when we make marriage a priority in the midst of a crazy, confusing world. Marriage is one of the easiest things we can allow to coast on cruise control before realizing it is headed in the wrong direction, or drifting aimlessly. Back up, turn it around, and get intentional about where you're going. Keep examining and readjusting the priorities. It's never too late to start enjoying marriage more as God intended for it to be enjoyed.

END NOTES

1. *The Show Must Go On*, written by Brian May and Queen, 1991.

Chapter 8

COMMUNICATE

"Do not let any unwholesome talk come out of your mouths, but only what is helpful for building others up according to their needs, that it may benefit those who listen."
—Ephesians 4:29

As we examine our priorities, certainly communication must be high on our list. Happiness in marriage is limited by the extent that we share our true self with our mate. How can we be friends if we do not talk, and how can we be lovers if we are not friends? Communication is challenging; communication between a man and a woman is doubly challenging, because we are so different! In fact, communication is a major problem in most marriages. Before marriage, we dream of finding that soul mate, the one to whom we can pour out our hearts and share our inmost thoughts. When we dated, we seemed to be able to talk about anything—the communication flowed. Often, in the midst of babies, work, church and life in general, that "flow" gets blocked. Communication takes effort, and after fifty-six years of marriage, we are still working on it. We have learned a lot, but we have found that excellent communication is a lifelong process.

BIBLICAL HELPS ABOUT COMMUNICATING

The Bible is full of instruction about good communication. Consider these verses among many others.

> *"...let every person be quick to hear, slow to speak..."* (James 1:19);

> *"Set a guard, O LORD, over my mouth; keep watch over the door of my lips!"* (Psalm 141:3)

"Let your speech always be gracious, seasoned with salt, so that you may know how you ought to answer each person." (Colossians 4:6)

"If one gives an answer before he hears, it is his folly and shame." (Proverbs 18:13)

"A fool takes no pleasure in understanding, but only in expressing his opinion." (Proverbs 18:2)

"The heart of the righteous ponders how to answer, but the mouth of the wicked pours out evil things." (Proverbs 15:28)

"Whoever guards his mouth preserves his life; he who opens wide his lips comes to ruin." (Proverbs 13:3)

"Let there be no filthiness nor foolish talk nor crude joking, which are out of place, but instead let there be thanksgiving." (Ephesians 5:4)

THE POWER OF NONVERBAL COMMUNICATION

There are two parts of communication: verbal and nonverbal. Our words, as well as our tones, sighs, body language, and even our silence speak volumes about what is in our heart. In the movie, *Fiddler on the Roof* there is a famous scene where the husband asks his wife if she loves him. She is shocked that he would even ask such a thing and replies that for twenty-five years of marriage she has cared for him, taken care of the house, made his bed, cooked his food, and reared their kids. And then she says, "If that isn't love then what it is?" That interaction illustrates how important words are. Considering all these things, it is understandable that there are many opportunities for miscommunication. When we talk, it is a challenge to accurately connect with our words. One of us can say something that the other doesn't hear, and the other can hear something that we didn't say.

Though subtler and less direct, some studies have shown that our nonverbal communication communicates more than ten times what our words do! Our tone of voice is a big factor in communication. A strong angry tone will probably cause the other to shut down or react. Proverbs 15:1 states that *"A gentle answer turns away wrath, but a harsh word stirs up anger."* Even with right words our tone can communicate disapproval, leading to defensiveness in the other. Inappropriate timing for a laugh can hurt our feelings and cause us to feel that we are being made fun of. We still remember one of our girls as a toddler in response to our laughter, crying and saying, "Not bery funny!"

At times I communicate resistance and hesitancy to Al with nothing more than a wordless sigh. Husbands have told us that their wives show disrespect to them through their looks and tone of voice. When we meet with a couple, we can tell a lot about the condition of their relationship before any words are spoken. If they are sitting far apart or one of them has his or her arms folded tightly, we can guess they are not communicating very well. A warning sign to Al in our communication is my silence, because I am a talker! Of course, there is a good and comfortable type of silence, but I'm talking about the "cold wall" of silence that blocks Al out. Even if I have a pleasant expression on my face, that silence screams loudly, "I am upset with you. I am not willing to talk about it right now. Leave me alone!"

MEN & WOMEN HEAR DIFFERENTLY

It is important to learn how differently we think. Early in our marriage we saw some of these differences as we argued from time to time as we misunderstood each other. It was not until several years later that we realized that many of our differences were not just our own quirks but are typical of most men and women. A book that conveyed this to us in a clever and informative way was John Gray's *Men Are from Mars, Women Are from Venus.*[1] Al read some of Gray's book before I did, and then I had a somewhat painful introduction to the principles about which he had been reading. He was putting Christmas boxes back on the shelves in the garage. I went out to help him and offered a few very helpful suggestions as to how he could do it better. He said, "Gloria, I will put the boxes away while you go read that book!" I left the job with him, but I felt aggravated and totally confused because I was only trying to help. After reading the book, I saw that my offering unsolicited help to Al communicated to him that I did not trust him to do the job correctly. Prior to that I would have thought he was just in a bad mood. Not many things undermine a man's confidence like his wife's unsolicited corrections and criticisms.

BE DIRECT

Men are problem-solvers by nature. They deal with problems by thinking silently, preferably in their "cave" as Gray describes it. Men tend to handle this problem-solving stress by watching TV, jogging or playing sports. Women, on the other hand, tend to solve problems by thinking out loud and talking through every aspect, big or small. The more we women talk, the better we feel, and eventually we see things more clearly. Complications arise when the wife brings up something as it comes to her mind. If it has a negative, "problem" sound, the problem-solving husband immediately feels responsible for the solution whether or not the wife asked for a solution.

More than a few times I have jumped in with a solution to a problem that Gloria is describing only to be told, "Don't try to fix it so fast; I just want you to listen!" Women, if you want your husband to hear what you are feeling or to simply discuss some issue, it helps to let us men know what you want. You might ask, "Is this a good time for us to talk? I would like to share some of my thoughts and feelings about...and just need a listening ear." That prepares us to listen rather than to going into our problem-solving mode.

Another aspect of our communication that needed to change was the way I asked questions. For example, I used to ask Al, "What time is the meeting?" Then I would be totally confused by his sometimes-irritated response. I learned to ask, "Do you know what time the meeting is?" My first question made Al feel that I expected him to have the answer. The second approach did not make him feel defensive. Sometimes rather simple adjustments on our part can make the difference between a good interaction and a fight. I don't always understand what the big deal is, but it certainly matters to him.

Another way of communicating I have had to change is my hinting. For example, I might mention to Al that the trash can is full, meaning that I would like him to empty it. He would much prefer that I just make a direct request as opposed to beating around the bush. I have also learned that it seems to make a difference if I say, "Will you?" versus "Can you?" I still do not fully understand that, but Al says for him it is true! As wives, we might find that when we ask, "Can you take out the trash?" our husbands might be tempted to say, "Yes, I can take it out. Do you want me to take it out?" So, be direct and don't try to soften a request by hinting at it.

HOW TO LISTEN

The ability to be a good listener is vital to effective communication. Real communication occurs when what is said is heard the way it was intended. Here are a few things that can help us be a better listener:

1. Look at the person doing the talking and maintain eye contact.

2. Don't interrupt.

3. Focus on what is being said. Since we process thoughts forty times faster than the other person can talk, it is very easy to be thinking of a response to what is being said or to just let our mind wander rather than really listening.

4. Restate what the other person just said to us. Statements such as "Let me see if I heard you correctly" and "Is this what you wanted me to hear?" are helpful tools.

DON'T LEAVE GAPS

A potential trap in communication is what is not said—gaps we leave in our communication. While it may take us a while to formulate our thoughts, we have learned that whatever gaps we leave in our communication with each other, Satan loves to fill. We usually assume the worst. Saying nothing is never taken as a compliment. If Gloria has to ask me how I think she looks, it's too late! She will probably assume that since I didn't say anything, I must not think she looks very good.

COMMUNICATING THROUGH PRAYER

Finally, nothing is more essential to effective communication in marriage than our relationship with God. In Solomon's oft-quoted statement, *"Two are better than one."* He ends the passage with, *"A cord of three strands is not quickly broken"* (Ecclesiastes 4:9-12). The most powerful "third strand" is God. From the beginning of our marriage, Al and I have prayed together daily. No one told us to do that; it just seemed like the right thing to do. We needed to actively involve God in our daily lives. Without realizing it at the time, we were drawing on the strength that we now refer to as the "spiritual glue of our marriage." We describe our prayer time as saying "good morning" and "good night" to God together.

We often find that we are very vulnerable in our prayers; and although we are talking to God, we are communicating powerfully with each other at the same time. There is no other specific input that we have given other couples more consistently or with more conviction than to pray together every day. In addition to our daily praying, we treasure prayer walks that are longer and more concentrated. We cannot imagine how difficult communication in any marriage would be without that which comes from a common foundation built on love for God and his Word.

None of us are or ever will be perfect communicators. It is a lifetime-to-learn skill that is vitally important to our functioning as one. May we work hard at becoming better and better at it and be gracious to each other as we try improve.

END NOTES _____

1. John Gray, *Men Are from Mars, Women Are from Venus: A Practical Guide for Improving Communication and Getting What You Want in Your Relationships* (HarperCollinsPublishers, 1992).

Chapter 9

FIGHT FAIRLY

"In your anger do not sin: Do not let the sun go down while you are still angry, and do not give the devil a foothold."
—Ephesians 4:26-27

No matter how hard we try to communicate correctly, communication at times is sure to go awry and end in conflict. Conflict is a part of life. We can't hide from it. But, why would we want to hide from conflict? Learning to resolve conflict in healthy ways helps us to grow as people and grow closer as a married couple.

I remember very well our first fight; it was on the second day of our honeymoon. We were driving to Cloudcroft, New Mexico, late in the evening. I was the driver and Gloria was the navigator with the map. Being the more adventurous one, I wanted to take a short cut and get us there more quickly and see some more beautiful mountain views along the way, against Gloria's better judgment. It turned out that she was right (as is often the case in our marriage); the shortcut turned out to be a very bumpy dirt road that didn't even show up on our map. To make things worse, we ran out of gas on that road; and it was a several-mile walk into town. That walk was not filled with "warm fuzzies." There was a chill in the air, and it was more than the falling temperature in the mountains as the sun was going down, and with us in short sleeves! There is more to the story, but we did make up. Being on our honeymoon, Gloria gave me a lot of grace, as she did for all our fifty-six years together!

In marriage, we are two different people trying to reflect God's oneness. We commit to resolving our conflicts because God calls us to unity.

Learning healthy conflict resolution is the challenge. Studies have shown that most couples do not successfully resolve their arguments. When a conflict is left unresolved the groundwork is already set for the next fight. Often it takes very little to set it off because of the issues that weren't previously settled. It is like continually sweeping dirt under a carpet—after a while the carpet has a bump in it where all the previous dirt has accumulated.

Before we even start the process of resolution, we need to agree on two ground rules. First, we will work through every conflict in real time. Second, certain things are NOT permitted at all; things like hitting, yelling, cursing, or anything else that would be completely out of bounds for a Christian.

In our many years together, we have come a long way in working through our conflicts, and have learned, through our mistakes, some things that work well and other things that don't work at all. In the past some of our fights would take several days to resolve completely; now it is very unusual for us to take more than five minutes to work through any disagreement. Several years ago, we decided to teach married couples what we have learned, and we entitled our guidelines, Ten Commandments for Fighting Fairly." This has probably helped more couples than anything else we have taught in our marriage classes and seminars. Here they are:

Ten Commandments for Fighting Fairly

1. **I am at fault. The percent doesn't matter.** None of our fights with each other has ever ended with one of us being totally right and the other totally wrong. Always there was at least some fault on both sides. At the end, both of us will have to own our part, even if we were only five per cent at fault. Knowing at the start that we will each have something to apologize for helps to keep us both humble as we work through our differences.

2. **Be more concerned with doing right than being right.** There is a real temptation for us to want to prove "our case" and win the fight, but the most important thing is to do right in God's eyes. In marriage conflicts there

is no such thing as "win-lose." It is always either "win-win" or "lose-lose." We need to remember that we are on the same team, and the only way to do that is for both of us to be on God's team. God gives us a directive that, if followed by both of us, will prevent most fights: *"Do everything without complaining or arguing..."* (Philippians 2:14). The easiest way to resolve a fight is to never start it in the first place.

3. **Don't use logic at emotional times.** Usually, one of us tends to be the more logical of the two. During conflict when emotions are high, trying to use logic is like pouring gasoline on a fire. There is a time for logic, but only after the emotions have cooled down.

4. **Assume and express love.** We call this "defining the boxing ring." In the heat of the battle, it is helpful to stop and say to each other, "This is not about my love for you; I really do love you." Things can get very heated in an argument, so it is helpful to know that the vitally important things in our marriage are not in question.

5. **Do not say never, always, hate, stupid, divorce, ugly, fat, idiot, etc.** As you learn from your past conflicts together, you will find that certain words or expressions really hurt and are unfair. Although we may not really mean those words and may later apologize for saying them, they can still leave scars and give Satan a foothold to plant seeds of doubt at vulnerable times in the future. Have a talk at a calm time and agree to ban those words from future fields of battle (or any other time). Also, words like "always" and "never" are counterproductive exaggerations, and only encourage the other one to think of the exceptions rather than dealing with the point being made.

6. **Don't argue about who said what. Take responsibility for what the other hears you say.** It is hard to accept what they say they heard rather than what I am sure that I said. Even though I have had good intentions and meant it differently, I need to own what was heard and

how it was heard. Good communication only happens when what was said is heard in the way that it was intended.

7. **First understand, then be understood. Take turns—no interruptions.** This first part is Habit 5 from Steven Covey's book, *7 Habits of Highly Effective People*.[1] It is one of the most difficult commandments for us. We so much want to be understood, that we want to share our side. But, when we first take the time and effort to understand where the other one is coming from, the conflict often is resolved even before it starts. It is both humorous and sad how many of our fights turned out to be simple misunderstandings about things that after clarification, we really agreed with. So that we can understand, we need to speak one at a time, and not be thinking about what to say next while the other is talking.

8. **Use "I" and "that makes me feel...", not "you."—Validate such as "Is this what you meant?" or "Let me tell you how I heard that."** "You" words are accusative, but "I" words express vulnerability. "You" words put us on the defensive and push the other one away, but "I" words draw us nearer and help us understand. No one likes to be put on the defensive with a "you did this" or "you said that." But it is much more difficult to argue that a person's feeling or perspective does not have some validity.

9. **Use timeouts. Agree on their length of time.** Sometimes we need to cool off or sort out what we are thinking or feeling or just pray. A timeout can be a valuable part of successfully resolving conflict. It should be agreed up front that either of us can at any point say, "I need a time out." (Not, "You need a time out!") This should not be a way to avoid the conflict. When a time a timeout is called for, the time for reengagement needs to be agreed on. It may be as short as a walk around the block, or as long as overnight. Late-night arguments should be avoided, if at all possible because exhaustion

> doesn't help resolution. Then it is often wise to both agree to continue the discussion the next day when both are rested.
>
> 10. **Ask for and give forgiveness.** We have an entire chapter in this book about forgiveness. But a fight is not over until both of us have acknowledged our part, ask each other for forgiveness for our part, and granted forgiveness to each other.

Time for a post—game analysis. Though not a part of our *Ten Commandments for Fighting Fairly,* a tool that has been incredibly helpful to us is a review of the conflict (similar to a "post–game analysis" in sports). First, a warning: this MUST NOT be done until the disagreement has been totally resolved all the way through Step 10. Then reviewing what happened, asking, "What could I have done differently to have helped the process of resolution?" and "How could we have avoided the conflict altogether?" We have learned so much about each other, understanding each other, our triggers, etc. and this has been a major tool for accomplishing this. Now, we very seldom have a real fight, and when we do it is usually resolved very quickly.

Any two people are going to have disagreements with each other if they are together for any length of time. Working through those times will determine the quality of the relationship. Unresolved differences will eventually poison a marriage but developing skills to have win-win disagreements will serve as a major building block in the kind of marriage that God and we want to have.

END NOTES _____

1. Gary Chapman and Jennifer Thomas, *The Five Languages of Apology* (Northfield Publishing, 2006).

Chapter 10

FORGIVE EVERYTHING

*"Let all bitterness and wrath and anger
and clamor and slander be put away
from you, along with all malice. Be kind
to one another, tenderhearted, forgiving
one another, as God in Christ forgave you."*
—Ephesians 4:31-32

Though we may learn to fight fairly, without forgiveness there is no true resolution. Marghanita Laski, a well-known atheist, made an amazing confession on television. She said, "What I envy most about you Christians is your forgiveness." She added, rather sadly, "I have no one to forgive me." But we are Christian couples who do have forgiveness from God, and we are committed to continually forgiving each other.

Infidelity, addiction and physical or emotional abuse are a few of the major causes of marriage failure. Some will have to face these challenges; we will discuss that more in a later chapter. All of us, however, face a much more subtle (and often even more dangerous) destructive force that can divide us, rob us of our joy, and eventually erode our love for each other; lack of forgiveness.

WE BOTH NEED FORGIVENESS

Most of us, when we are dating, marvel at how much we are alike; we liked the same music, food, movies, sports, etc. But it doesn't take long after the honeymoon to see just how different we really are, and many of these differences can turn into annoyances; he leaves the toilet seat up, she never gets gas for the car, he leaves his dirty underwear on the floor, she is always late. The list goes on. It can be these smaller irritants, and our negative responses to them, that kill the warm, loving feelings between us. Marriage is the union of two imperfect people who make lots of mistakes. When we are in a relationship with someone, chances are one hundred percent that both of us will mess up, be selfish and hurt each another—sometimes by accident and sometimes on purpose. Without forgiveness, these differences can turn into grudges between us that over time will erode the relationship.

LACK OF FORGIVENESS DESTROYS EQUALITY

Forgiveness includes those major hurts and sins against one another, but it also includes forgiving things like unintentional slights, forgetfulness and those parts of each other's personality that drive you crazy (and may never change). Each of these types of forgiveness is important in a successful marriage but becoming more and more forgiving toward your partner is critical. Forgiving a specific wrong reduces the stress and hostility that stems from an unresolved hurt but becoming a truly forgiving husband or wife creates a marriage that goes beyond what you ever hoped it could be.

When you decide to really forgive your partner, you open the door to a real love affair. We miss out when we spend our lives criticizing our mates and complaining about all the ways they don't measure up to our standards. When we fail to forgive, unequal relationships develop. True closeness becomes an impossibility because the "offended" is in a position of holding the "offender" in prison, and the obsession with being wronged and seeking revenge holds the victim in prison as well. The one who made the mistake or hurt the other is kept in a "one down" position of being indebted to the other.

LACK OF FORGIVENESS ERODES THE LOVE BOND

Lack of forgiveness slowly eats away at the love bond in marriage, and the damage may go unnoticed for a long time. The disastrous effects can be like what happened to the great composer Ludwig van Beethoven. For nearly two centuries, Beethoven's death was a mystery. He had suffered from irritability, depression, abdominal pain and finally death. In 1994, two Americans launched a study to determine his cause of death. Chemical analysis of a strand of his hair revealed his killer: lead poisoning.[1] More than likely, it was just a little poison in everyday activities that took his life. It could have come from drinking out of lead lined cups or having dinner on a lead lined plate—both common household items in that day. It didn't come in one lump sum, but the lead killed him slowly and quietly, one little bit of poison at a time. That's how lack of forgiveness resulting in bitterness can destroy a marriage.

Little by little, day by day, we can allow bitterness to poison us. Our mate will do something upsetting, and instead of confronting and resolving the problem, we can silently hold it against them. They continue to make the same mistakes, and we continue to harbor resentment, and our marriage slowly dies.

CHARACTERISTICS OF FORGIVENESS

So, what is forgiveness all about? Let's look at some of its characteristics.

1. Forgiveness is a condition of my eternal salvation (Matthew 6:14-15). If I don't forgive, neither will God forgive me.

2. While forgiveness will help my mate and my marriage, it first and foremost will help me. My forgiving someone, frees me. My lack of forgiveness holds me prisoner and leads to my own pain, anger, bitterness, and resentment. Left unchecked these feelings can potentially become emotionally, mentally, verbally, or physically disastrous. People who don't forgive typically have higher heart rates and blood pressure and other physical problems. Countless studies show blame, stress and anger can cause or worsen diseases, such as cancer, heart disease, and various auto-immune disorders.

3. Forgiveness is an action, not a feeling. If I wait until I feel like forgiving, that may never happen. Rather, it is a decision that is based on God's command; an action that is not conditional and it does not depend on how much my partner understands my hurt or even if they are sorry or not. There is no "I'll forgive you if...'you promise to never do it again,' or 'if you'll clean the house,' or 'you agree to get help'" or any other conditions I may come up with.

4. Forgiveness is a process, not an event. It might take some time to work through my emotions before I can truly forgive. It may be like peeling the layers of an onion. As soon as I can, I should decide to forgive, but it may not happen immediately in the case of much more serious sins, such as adultery. Sometimes we want to "hurry up" and forgive so the pain will end, or so we can get along with our mate, but we must be careful not to simply cover our wounds and retard the healing process. Maybe all I can offer now is, "I want to forgive you, but right now I'm struggling emotionally. I promise I will work on it." When that happens, I need to get help from others who are qualified to help me to work through things.

5. Forgiveness is not pretending that everything is okay. Some fear that if I forgive my offender, they are let off the hook scot-free and get to go about their merry way while I unfairly suffer from their actions. It is not saying or thinking "Don't worry about what you did, I'm fine with it and we all make mistakes." That may sound spiritual and great coming out of my mouth, but inside I will probably be struggling with hypocrisy. Instead, forgiveness is giving God the right to dispense justice, not me. By refusing to transfer the right of judgment to God, I am telling him that I don't trust him to take care of matters. But neither is forgiveness letting the offense happen again and again; I don't have to tolerate abuse. We still may need help in our reconciliation or with establishing healthier patterns and dynamics.

6. Forgiveness is not the same as forgetting what happened. It's normal for memories to be triggered in the future. When thoughts of past hurts occur, it's what I do with them that counts. The real goal is to get to the point that I remember the incident but don't relive the feelings. Forgiveness is refusing to remind my mate of how he or she has wronged me or wanting to cause the same kind of pain that I've been caused and refusing

to bring up the matter in a harmful way. That means, for example, no subtle digs and not using it as a trump card in the next argument. And talking to others about the incident probably means that I'm still nursing my memory of the offense.

7. When I am the one who needs forgiveness, I need to help rather than hurt the healing process. The first thing that I need to do is to understand what I did (or didn't do) that hurt my mate. Then I need to ask God to help me be humble enough to take responsibility for my part. Gary Chapman has written a very helpful book, *The Five Languages of Apology,*[2] with very practical suggestions. They are a) express regret; "I am sorry for...", b) accept responsibility; "I know what I did was wrong", c) make restitution; "what can I do to make it right?", d) genuinely repent; "I will try not to do that again", and e) ask for forgiveness; "will you forgive me?" We have found this to be very helpful in resolving our marriage bumps.

Here are a few other things that have helped us in working through forgiveness:

1. Remember that I chose this relationship and made a life-long commitment to it, so I need to do my part in making it a success.

2. Realize we are both sinners and continually in need of God's forgiveness.

3. Accept the non-sinful things in my mate that probably will never change, such as personality traits.

4. Remember that Satan is the enemy, not each other. Satan is a master at making us forget that.

5. Focus on what I am thankful for in my mate. In the heat of the moment it is hard to remember all the positive things that drew us together. Beautiful roses also have thorns.

6. No matter how hopeless it may seem at the time, with God's help and plan we can work through our difficulties and grow even closer together.

As author Ruth Bell Graham said, "A happy marriage is the union of two good forgivers!"

END NOTES _____

1. Martha Irvine, "Beethoven's Hair Has Signs of Poisoning" October 17, 2000, https://abcnews.go.com/Technology/story?id=119868&page=1.

Chapter 11

ALWAYS BE THANKFUL

"Be joyful always; pray continually;
give thanks in all circumstances,
for this is God's will for you in Christ Jesus."
—1 Thessalonians 5:16-18

Now that we have tools for forgiveness, we can learn to go further and deeper in our relationships. A grateful heart changes our perspective on most things in our relationships.

It is so interesting that the two of us can be at the same event and leave with totally different impressions. We can go through similar life experiences and have them affect us in radically different ways. The fact is that in our search for happiness and fulfilment, each of us sees and experiences the world through our own unique lens, and our lens makes all the difference. We don't see things as they are; rather we see them as we are. The verse quoted above contains three of the shortest commands in the whole Bible, and they are probably the most disobeyed three commands in the entire Bible. In this chapter, we will focus on the last of the three: giving thanks. (We will use "thankfulness" and "gratitude" interchangeably.)

Thankfulness is the lens that will totally change the way we see God, ourselves, our marriage, and the circumstances of life.

We don't just wake up one day as thankful people; we were not born being thankful. Neither is it one of the gifts of the Holy Spirit as listed in Galatians 5. Rather, it is something that we must work on, exercise and grow in. And as it grows, our perception of reality changes. And as our thankfulness grows, we see our marriage more and more as one of God's greatest gifts.

Under the Mosaic Law of the Old Testament there were two types of sacrifices: sacrifices that were required at specific times and for specific reasons and sacrifices that were totally left up to individuals to offer whenever they were moved to do so. One these "free-will" offerings was the "thank offering", sacrificed at any time for no other reason than to thank God for some particular thing. Psalm 50:23 (GNV) states, "*Giving thanks is the sacrifice that honors me.*" So, having a spirit of thanksgiving is clearly very important to God.

But how can we be thankful "in all circumstances"? This sounds impossible. We have lost three babies. Our first child was a boy who lived only three days. Our third and fourth were twin girls who just lived one day. Six years ago, Gloria was diagnosed with stage-four cancer. Those were and still are some of the most difficult times of our lives; how can we be thankful?

First, we have learned that the command is not to be thankful "for all circumstances" but "in all circumstances." We were not thankful for the difficult situations themselves but have since come to the point that we can list many good things that resulted from or were directly involved with those very hard things. This is possible only by our faith in God. He has made an incredible promise in Romans 8:28: "*And we know that in all things God works for the good of those who love him, who have been called according to his purpose.*" The promise is not that "in some things" God works for our good, but "in all things!" Without the confidence that God will keep that promise, it would be impossible to be thankful in the many difficult situations that we all face in our lives.

With the belief that God has every one of our challenges under control, how can we not be thankful to him? But knowing we should thank him and remembering to think about it and actually thank him every day are two different things. Without the conviction and some type of a plan, we can go for a long time without having that God-awareness.

In our lens analogy, there are only two possible choices for the lens through which we see life: gratitude or ingratitude. Psychologist and author Dr. Henry Cloud, in his book *The Law Of Happiness*,[1] states that amazingly only ten percent of our happiness actually comes from anything having to do with our circumstances. He states that whether we are rich or poor, get the job we want or don't, are sick or healthy, etc., we get only a ten percent jump in our happiness when something circumstantial goes well. The other ninety percent depends on the lens we are looking through. "Happy people, and this is scientific research," he says, "do not compare themselves to others." Further adding, "The opposite of envy is gratitude." We all know people who have everything that it would take to be happy, and they are not happy, because they want something else or they want more of the same. And we all know people who have terrible circumstances that we are thankful we don't have, and they are very happy. They radiate happiness. Why? Because they are grateful. So, it is not happiness that makes us grateful. It's gratefulness that makes us happy.

We certainly don't always look through the right lens, but here is an illustration of what we are talking about. In our five-plus decades together we have lived in five states, multiple cities, and many different communities. So, a common question we are asked is "where is the favorite place you have lived?" We can honestly say that every place we have lived is our favorite place. In every place there were positives and negatives, great things that happened and hard things. We just try to focus on the great things and leave the hard things to God. Being thankful really works, and it is a much happier way to live.

As is always the case, God's blessings accompany obedience to his commands. A study was conducted by psychologists Michael McCollough (Southern Methodist University) and Robert Emmons (University of California)[2] on the act of gratitude. The study broke people into three groupsand the members of all three groups were asked to keep a journal. The first group kept a journal on events that happened during their day, regardless of good or bad; the second group was asked to record unpleasant experiences; the last was asked to make a list daily of things they were grateful for. The results of the study showed that the daily gratitude group had higher reported levels of alertness, energy, determination and optimism. Also, the group expressed less stress, anxiety and depression, exercised more and achieved more goals that they set.

In addition to thanking God, being thankful for each other is one of the most important parts of keeping our marriage alive and exciting. Too often we take for granted the very things that most deserve our gratitude. As marriages move past the honeymoon stage, couples go from appreciating and loving every little detail about each other to taking each other for granted. We can get so used to having our mate in our life that we forget why we chose to be with them. We become deadened to their special qualities and instead focus on things that annoy us about them and wonder what happened to that magic spark.

Gratitude is vital part of any healthy and enduring relationship, but it takes consistent effort to keep it fresh and sincere. It helps us remember the reasons that we fell in love with each other in the first place; it increases our love, fun, and forgiveness, and it deepens our spiritual intimacy. Gratitude enhances sex; true mutual thankfulness deepens our emotional and spiritual bonds, which inevitably create a more intense physical connection. Gratitude creates a mutual cycle of appreciation. It's interesting that when we feel appreciated by our mate, we're more likely to show them appreciation too.

Practicing gratitude in marriage can have a snowball effect because as one partner expresses thanks and affirmation, the same comes flowing back from the other. The goal is for us to create a permanent culture of gratitude. Remember together. Enjoy reflecting on memories and seasons that you've shared (See Chapter 21 on memories). Be grateful for the journey you've walked together so far, stating appreciation for one another and for the shared experiences. Say "thank you," even for the small things. A "thank you" for washing the dog, washing the car, for taking out the trash, for making the bed, for cooking dinner. Even small gestures of gratitude, build and sustain an atmosphere of love and appreciation.

Gratitude helps to soften our negative interactions. Constructive criticism and correction are not necessarily ingratitude. Certainly, there are times that we must address unpleasant things in our relationship. Harsh words sting and can easily have the power to tear down confidence in our marriage. Significantly, studies by marriage researcher John Gottman show than if the number of negative comments and interactions is too large compared to the positive ones, the marriage can be severely damaged or destroyed. He found that, over time, in order to have a healthy relationship, at least five positive comments are needed for every negative one. For couples where the long-term positives are less than the negatives, divorce is likely. We must work hard to ensure that our positive interactions far outweigh our negative ones.

Ingratitude makes it very difficult to enjoy the here-and-now. When we were poor graduate-school students at the University of Texas it was a temptation to dwell on how little we had and how much our circumstances would improve when we finally enjoyed a PhD salary. We ate lots of beans-and-cornbread, Spam, and Vienna sausages. (Once we even bought a can of imitation Vienna sausages, but they looked and smelled like dog food, so we decided we were not that poor!) In retrospect, those years gave us some of our most special memories; we had very little materially, but we had each other and were deeply in love (and still are).

Giving thanks for and with our mate is one of the most significant habits we can build into our marriage. Some have found it helpful to keep what they call a gratitude journal where each day they write the things that have given them significant pleasure, comfort, love, laughter, or any other positive feeling. Whatever works for you, do it, because there is ALWAYS something to be thankful for. And giving thanks pleases God and helps keep our marriage fresh and alive.

END NOTES

1. Henry Cloud, *The Law of Happiness* (Simon & Schuster, 2011).

2. Robert Emmons and Michael McCullough (2003). "Counting Blessings Versus Burdens: An Experimental investigation of Gratitude and Subjective Well-Being in Daily Life." *Journal of Personality and Social Psychology*, 84, 377-389. doi:10.1037/0022-3514.84.2.377.

Chapter 12

ENCOURAGE EACH OTHER

"Two are better than one,
because they have a good
return for their labor:
If either of them falls down,
one can help the other up.
But pity anyone who falls
and has no one to help them up."
—Ecclesiastes 4:9-10

When we arc thankful for each other and are best friends, then we can become each other's cheer leader. Life is filled with ups and downs, and so is marriage. Research shows that a vital characteristic of an exciting, successful relationship is that both the husband and wife regularly encourage each another. We shouldn't need research to tell us that. The importance of cncouragement is emphasized repeatedly in the Bible. Ephesians 4:29 tells us, *"Do not let any unwholesome talk come out of your mouths, but only what is helpful for building others up according to their needs, that it may benefit those who listen."* 1 Thessalonians 5:11 says, *"Therefore encourage one another and build each other up, just as in fact you are doing."* And, Hebrews 3:13 commands, *"But encourage one another daily, as long as it is called Today, so that none of you may be hardened by sin's deceitfulness."*

The word encouragement, literally translated from Greek, means to inspire with courage. From the Bible, we find that encouragement can come from several places. First it comes directly from God (Psalms 10:17; Romans 15:5) and from the Bible (Romans 15:4). This is one reason that we repeatedly emphasize a deep relationship with God throughout this book. Who better to get our courage from than God? Then, having solid Christian friends who know us well and who pray for us are sources of great encouragement. But, next to God, no one can encourage me like Gloria—her words, her look, her faith in me, her touch, and her example.

In this chapter we are going to explore some ways that we can effectively encourage each other as husband and wife. The things we discuss here are not in any particular order.

1. Learn what encourages your partner. In order to give the kind of encouragement that really counts, we must first understand each other. Each of us brings to marriage a unique set of needs and backgrounds. Even though we may love each other and have the best of intentions, we are effective only as we come to understand each other's needs. We refer to Gary Chapman's insightful book, *The 5 Love Languages*[1] several times throughout our book. He explains how to show love to your mate and describes five ways to do so: words of affirmation, acts of service, receiving gifts, quality time, and physical touch. Gloria's love language is words of affirmation, mine are quality time and physical touch. Understanding these "love languages" about each other gives us a head start in knowing where to start with our encouragement.

2. Learn what discourages your partner, and steer clear of that as much as is possible. If we're not careful, we can focus on the one thing that's wrong and be much slower to point out the many things that are right. Focusing on our mate's faults can be highly toxic to our marriage. Does that mean we should never point out needs in each other's lives? Of course not. We all need honest input from each other. But our ability to give humble, helpful critique and have it well received depends on how much effective encouragement we are giving overall. As we cited earlier, author John Gottman states that marriages operate best when spouses communicate at least five positive comments for every negative one. He found that the average ratio for divorced couples was three positive comments for every four negative ones. Remember that encouragement

needs to be unconditional. We may think we are being encouraging by saying something positive but adding a "but..." to the comment. "I love it when you cook, but ... I wish you wouldn't make such a mess;" or "Thank you for putting your dirty clothes in the hamper, why don't you do that all the time?" Encouragement tied to a condition counts as a discouragement.

3. Anticipate challenging times that your mate may be facing and pray for the wisdom to be helpful. One husband of a young family was planning to ask his boss for a desperately-needed raise. His wife prayed hard for her husband's plans and decided to prepare a special candlelight dinner to be served when he got home. He greeted her at the door with the great news that he got the raise. They sat down to dinner, and he found a card in an envelope on his plate. He opened the card and read, "Congratulations, darling! You have worked so hard, and I believed you would get the raise! You deserve it. This evening will show you how much I love you." Needless to say, it was a great evening. The next day, the husband was taking out the trash can, and he noticed an unopened card in the can. He opened it and read, "I am so sorry, darling. Don't worry about not getting the raise. You worked so hard and really deserved it. I'm sure you will get one soon. This evening will show you how much I love you." Regardless of whether he got the raise or not, she had planned a way to encourage her man! She understood encouragement.

4. Being thankful for each other is encouraging. Together thank God for orchestrating your relationship. So many things could have happened differently that would have prevented you from even meeting each other. Gloria and I were enrolled at the same time in a relatively small Christian college (three thousand students) but didn't know each other. She somehow became interested in getting to know me. There was a campus event where most students brought a date.

Gloria had decided that if I was there without a date, she was going to ask me out later. If I had a date, she wasn't going to pursue it any farther. I was supposed to have a date with another girl, but she had cancelled, so I went without a date. Gloria asked me out, and the rest is history. If my date had not cancelled, Gloria and I would not have had 56 magical years together! We feel that God had his hand in those events, and we often thank him for putting us together.

5. Resolve to change the things that bother your mate. There are times that I use an angry tone with Gloria. The tone often causes Gloria to shut down emotionally. I know when she gets quiet that I have messed up. This had been a problem in our marriage for years. A part of the problem is that I am not usually aware of even having the tone. Because of how I saw that it hurt her, I asked her to tell me immediately when I used the tone. By working together, the tone now happens much less frequently. Gloria, on the other hand, had a problem with being late. It would be time for us to go somewhere, and she would not be ready. She saw how much that bothered me and asked me to tell her fifteen minutes before time to leave so she could be sure and be ready. This plan helped solve the lateness problem. While these were not monumental problems for either of us, the fact that each of us is willing make the effort to change is encouraging to each other.

6. Find at least one thing to praise your mate for every day. Be creative in how you express your praise. A simple face-to-face thank you, a text, a card, a phone call, a letter in the mail, a flower, a hug, a massage, a present, a surprise get-away, an invitation to the bedroom— you get the point. Make encouragement fun. What if each of you were so creative and regular in your encouragement, that each day you wondered how the next encouragement would be delivered?

7. Does your mate know that you think they are attractive? The lover in Song of Songs tells his love, *"Behold, you are*

beautiful, my beloved, truly delightful." (Song of Songs 1:16), and she in other places praises his physical qualities. We all crave appreciation. What were some of the physical characteristics in your mate that first attracted you? They probably look a bit different today than when you married, ours certainly do now that we are in our seventies. But there are things about Gloria that are just as physically attractive as ever; her beautiful blue eyes, her warm, radiant smile and other things that I won't mention. We all want to know that we are valued and loved, pursued and special. When is the last time you shared some things that you find physically attractive about your mate? Whatever it is, share it! It will be encouraging.

8. For most of us, the area in which we tend to be most insecure is our sexual relationship. Let's get practical here. Is your mate a good lover? Have you told them so? Be specific. Let them know what pleases you and when. Hollywood, Television, and the Internet have so distorted what is realistic in the bedroom, that it is easy to feel inadequate. Success in bed should be totally determined by what pleases and excites the two of you. Working together along with good communication should bring fulfillment for both husband and wife. Gloria and I find that we improve with time, because we learn better what pleases each other. A huge part of getting better is mutually encouraging each other. We both know when we have had a great time together, and we don't let each other forget it.

9. The single most encouraging thing in our life is our relationship with God. Everything else in our marriage is shaped by him and his standards. The peace and confidence that comes from knowing that both of us have the same standards make all the difference as we navigate the uncharted waters of raising a family, getting older, and facing health challenges.

God has equipped us in marriage with some very powerful tools; through his spirit we have more power than we even know. Among the most powerful is encouragement. With encouragement, whether through a word, an attitude, expressing hope for the future, the knowledge of being prayed for, the interaction of praying together, demonstrating confidence in God, being loved unconditionally despite not being perfect, or being supported by your mate in life's challenges, we can fill each other with faith, strength and energy.

END NOTES

1. Gary Chapman, *The Five Love Languages* (Zondervan, 1995).

Chapter 13

HAVE REALISTIC EXPECTATIONS

"All relationships have the same basic components: people, needs and expectations."
—Iyanla Vanzant

"Expectation is the root of all heartache."
—Shakespeare

Regardless of how much we may try to encourage each other, at times we can be surprised by unmet expectations.

Marriage is challenging because each of us brings our long list of expectations that have been built over years, and we must decide how to mesh both sets together. Not only are we unaware of the expectations that the other is bringing to the marriage, we often are not even aware of all the ones that we have! Problems develop in our marriage whenever we assume our mate shares our expectations. When something doesn't go the way we think it should, we feel frustrated, disappointed, and even angry.

As adults, we have all lived long enough to have established certain tastes and values in our lives. It is important for us to identify, not only what our expectations are, but where they come from. Our family background plays a large part in building our expectations. We may assume that everyone does something a certain way because that's how it was done in our family. Other expectations come from our own experiences, our friends, our past relationships, social media, television and movies, magazine articles, and the like.

Everyone has expectations, but they are very tricky things. The dictionary definition tells us that expectations are either believing something is going to happen or believing something should be a certain way. We have purposely included two quotes with different views at the start of this chapter, because different perspectives on expectations in marriage range all the way from "if you don't have any expectations, you will never be disappointed" to there is no meaningful relationship that doesn't have some expectations attached. So, it should come as no surprise that there are different types of expectations, some are helpful, and some are destructive.

In this chapter we want to examine some expectations that can hurt our marriage and some that can help it.

UNREASONABLE EXPECTATIONS

Some expectations are not only unreasonable, but are also dangerous, because they cannot or should not be met. When expectations are not met over time, they lead to frustration, conflict, disappointment and even failure of the marriage.

Here are a few bad expectations:

1. I expect my mate to meet all my needs.

First of all, focusing on my own needs can ruin a marriage. Secondly, only God is able to meet all of my needs.

2. I expect marriage to make me happy.

It is easy to turn marriage into a personal idol, believing that the "perfect spouse" is my source of happiness in life. This expectation places an incredible pressure on any spouse. No spouse is perfect, and no person can be my single source of happiness. We once tried to help a couple where the wife used Psalm 37:4, *"Take delight in the LORD, and he will give you the desires of your heart"* to force her husband to buy her whatever she wanted whenever she wanted it. She once said God would like for her husband to buy her a fur coat because Jesus wants him to make her happy! Only Jesus can give lasting happiness. (See Chapter 14 on happiness and joy)

3. I thought my mate would change after we got married.

Marrying someone with the expectation they will become a different person after marriage is unreasonable and unfair. Marriage is not a magic change agent that transforms a person. My job is to work to love, accept and understand the person I married.

4. I thought marriage would be easy.

Having a successful marriage requires our dependence on

God and our lifelong effort. It takes real work to understand a spouse and honor and love him or her. Life and marriage will have some hard times.

UNRESOLVED EXPECTATIONS

We enter marriage thinking we know and understand each other, only to discover there are lots of yet-to-be-discovered expectations that we didn't even think of. These expectations are not necessarily good or bad; but until they are worked through, they are problems waiting to happen and these are unresolved expectations. They include such things as how we spend money, how often we will make love, how many children we will have, where we will spend holidays, whether we will buy new or used cars and how much we will spend on them, who cleans the house, who cooks, and who handles yard work. Looking back, even the happiest of couples will acknowledge that these "little" unspoken expectations have created tension in their marriage.

I have always been a stickler for being on time for any event that has a stated starting time; Gloria, not so much and that frequently caused friction between us. A weekly Bible study group that we led had a very distinguished visitor for several weeks: Camelia Sadat, the daughter of slain Egyptian president and Nobel Peace Prize winner Anwar Sadat. When Camelia attended, she was often late because of her busy schedule. That never bothered me at all; I was just thrilled to have such a prominent person attending. Then one day my hypocrisy hit me; an important person could be late and it not bother me, but the most important person in my life, Gloria, could be late and I would be upset with her. I apologized to Gloria for holding her to a standard that I didn't hold others to. I was able to verbalize why being on time was so important to me. Gloria recognized the value of timeliness to me and decided to work on making it a priority for herself to encourage me and to help us grow in our unity.

UNSPOKEN EXPECTATIONS

Of all the problems that come from expectations, the most common are those that have not been discussed—they are unspoken, so they come as a surprise. In pre-marriage counseling we do with engaged couples, one thing we are sure to do is to discuss their expectations about the upcoming honeymoon. It is not unusual for the woman to envision some time shopping, eating at nice restaurants and sightseeing as well as time together in the bedroom. The guy, on the other hand, typically pictures non-stop love making. This is clearly a set up for a disappointing honeymoon. Talking through these unspoken expectations can really help the couple to prepare for an exciting, memory-making first few days together.

In our travels, one trip to Europe included a week of driving in incredibly beautiful Switzerland. We arrived a little before sunset in an enchanting little mountain village called Kusnacht. And then came a fight that totally ruined our evening in paradise. Gloria was hungry, so she was eager to go eat, or so I thought. There was a beautiful sunset, so I wanted us to have a romantic walk and enjoy the sunset hand-in-hand. Gloria kept talking about being hungry, so I angrily gave in to what I thought she wanted. We ate what would have normally been a very romantic and memorable meal at an exceptionally good restaurant. It was a memorable meal all right. Memorable because we were both miserable and very upset with each other.

As we worked through our fight the next day, we learned a very important lesson about the danger of unspoken expectations. Gloria had wanted to enjoy the sunset, too; she just wanted to make sure that the restaurant would be open after our walk. I wrongly assumed that she had wanted to eat rather than enjoy the sunset, so I angrily insisted that we go eat immediately. If we had only taken the time to say what each us was feeling and thinking, both of us would have been very happy, and each of our expectations would have been met. To this day, we only have to mention the word "Kusnacht," and we both sadly shake our heads, remembering what could have been, but also very thankful for the lesson we learned about unspoken expectations.

GOOD EXPECTATIONS

Certainly, there is a long list of expectations that should be a part of any healthy Christian marriage. Here are few of the ones we think are most important:

1. God and the Bible will be the bottom-line standard for our marriage.

2. We will be faithful to each other; our marital love is reserved for only each other.

3. We will be together until death separates us.

4. We will choose to trust each other and give each other the benefit of the doubt.

5. We will always work to have open, honest communication with each other.

6. We will always try to express our love for each other physically, emotionally and spiritually.

7. We will respect each other.

8. We will spend quality time together.

MOVING FORWARD

Let's close this chapter with a godly plan to recognize and reduce unmet expectations:

1. Start by praying together and putting Paul's words into action: *"Do nothing from selfish ambition or conceit, but in humility count others more significant than yourselves. Let each of you look not only to his own interests, but also to the interests of others."* Philippians 2:3-4 (ESV)

2. Verbalize your expectations as well as your partner's.

3. Try to see each other's perspective. Validate your mate's perspective and acknowledge that it is not necessarily better or worse than yours, it is just different, and that's okay.

4. Decide what compromises you can and cannot make.

5. And finally, find a solution that you both can accept.

Marriage is all about learning each other's expectations and then working to meet them. Satan will do all that he can to, as Shakespeare suggested, turn our expectations into heartaches. If we learn to avoid the unreasonable expectations, to embrace the good expectations, and to work through our unresolved expectations, we will be well on the way to building a fulfilling marriage together. These practices will lead us toward a happy marriage.

Chapter Fourteen

UNDERSTAND HAPPINESS AND JOY

*"But may the righteous be glad
and rejoice before God;
may they be happy and joyful."*
—Psalm 68:3

We have discussed the dangers of certain expectations. Unreasonable expectations about happiness can lead us to some unhealthy places.

I (Gloria) am Nonna to all my grandchildren. One day I was babysitting our first grandchild, Kiara. She was about two years old and had a mind of her own. On this particular day, Kiara was being stubborn, and nothing was pleasing her. Finally, I told her, "Kiara, you need to start obeying Nonna right now, or you can go and sit in your chair in your room." She continued her pouting, so I took her to her room, sat her down and said, "Kiara, you sit there until you get happy!" From the other room, I heard her sobbing defiantly, "My not happy! My not happy! My not happy!" A while later, Kiara came to me and said, "Nonna, my happy now!" A little time, reflection, and confinement helped her get to a better spot. Kiara is now in her mid-twenties, and we all still laugh about that day. Our struggle to be happy begins at an early age! And, we can carry that struggle into our marriage.

Nearly everyone wants to be happy. Aristotle, the ancient Greek philosopher, taught that the goal, central purpose, and 'supreme good' of human life is happiness. Our Declaration of Independence has as probably its best-known phrase, "Life, Liberty and the pursuit of Happiness." Most Americans surveyed say that their number one goal in life is to be happy.

SOLOMON'S SCIENTIFIC SEARCH FOR HAPPINESS

What almost everyone thinks in their pursuit of happiness

is "When I reach this goal or obtain this, then I'll be happy." As we write this chapter, the amount of money in the national lottery is approaching a record-breaking two billion dollars! Who of us cannot imagine the happiness that winning that lottery would bring? King Solomon, the son of David, was given the gift of wisdom from God (Read about it in 1 Kings and 2 Chronicles). In the book of Ecclesiastes, he describes his pursuit of happiness almost as a scientific experiment. He was a powerful, rich, intelligent king who set out on a quest for happiness and describes for us the results and conclusions of his lifelong experiment.

He amassed wealth amounting to multiple billions of dollars. He became a master builder of mind-blowing architectural projects. He tried wine as his source of happiness; today, we would broaden this to drugs. He tried sex; he had seven hundred wives and three hundred concubines. He became an academic, studying psychology, botany, and biology. He brought into his palace all the most popular entertainment.

In short, he tried everything he could think of to make him happy. At the end of it all, he wrote, *"Yet when I surveyed all that my hands had done and what I had toiled to achieve, everything was meaningless, a chasing after the wind."* (Ecclesiastes 2:11). He uses "meaningless" thirty-one time in Ecclesiastes! He closes his experiment with the conclusion that any effort to find happiness which doesn't put God first is doomed to failure.

SETTING PROPER PRIORITIES

Wanting to be happy is not a bad thing, if it is given the proper priority. It becomes bad if we want it more than anything else. Then we make the pursuit of happiness an idol, as it becomes more important than pursuing God. The problem with happiness as a goal is that it doesn't last very long. People can invest their whole lives chasing 'the dog's tail' in the mere pursuit of a few happy moments. And, if you ask a hundred people, you'll probably find at least a hundred different ideas of how to find happiness. About the only thing we can all agree on is that we want to be happy all the time, and most of us would say we want everyone else to be happy, too. But we live in a world filled with unhappiness. A recent Harris poll finds that only one third of Americans are happy. That is a depressingly low number with only one out of three of us getting what we want.

"And they lived happily ever after." That is the way fairy tales end, and therefore how we assume our marriage should be. A major problem in marriage can be the priority that we put on happiness. Too many people believe that marriage is supposed to make them happy. Anyone getting married with their own happiness as their main goal will be disappointed. Marriage is not about our happiness, it's not even about us. It's about love—which is something we choose to give time and time again. It's about sacrifice, serving, giving, forgiving—and then doing it all over again. Mostly, it is about God. Having bought into the world's lie that marriage is primarily about being happy, couples panic at the reality of their own relationship breaking under the stress of sickness, disappointment, sin, and the dailiness of life. As a result, many now get divorced for no other reason than they are not happy.

When we turn marriage into an idol of happiness, we are doomed to failure. Instead, let us consider the question that American evangelist Francis Chan rightly poses, "What if God designed marriage to make us holy more than to make us happy?" This question should help us examine our expectations. Instead of selfishness and accusation, consider asking these questions that lead to spirituality and intimacy:

1. "How is God reshaping my soul while teaching me to love my mate?"

2. "How does marriage confront my selfishness, and so help me to become more like Jesus, the servant of all?"

3. "How does marriage teach me to listen, instead of tuning out, and be gentle, instead of harsh, when my mate fails to meet my expectations?"

Satan has lied to us: marriage will collapse under our expectations if we weigh it down under the world's unrealistic ideas of happiness. But if we see marriage as a process of growing in intimacy and character, then the very things that most frustrate us about marriage can become stepping stones to intimacy and maturity. Instead of asking whether our marriage is making us happy, let us start asking how it is making us holy, and then thank God for his gift of marriage.

Unhappiness in your marriage is not a sign that you married the wrong person, or that you should leave your mate. Even amid struggles, a great marriage (and the resulting happiness) is possible with God's grace and hard work. It would be easy to blame our unhappiness on things like not spending enough quality time together, allowing bitterness and resentment to build in our hearts, or on communication issues. But while quality time, forgiveness, and good communication are vitally important for building and maintaining a happy marriage, if these things aren't happening, it is often a sign of a much deeper problem. And until this problem is solved, no amount of "fixing" will work.

Consider this Bible passage: *"One of them, an expert in the law, tested him with this question: 'Teacher, which is the greatest commandment in the Law?' Jesus replied: 'Love the Lord your God with all your heart and with all your soul and with all your mind.' This is the first and greatest commandment. And the second is like it: 'Love your neighbor as yourself.' All the Law and the Prophets hang on these two commandments."* (Matthew 22:35-40) Most every marital problem can be traced back to one or both partners failing to obey these two commandments.

The minute we begin to focus on our own happiness over those of God or our partner; there will inevitably be problems. Are you experiencing communication problems in your marriage? How often do you really focus on listening to what your partner (or God) has to say instead of insisting on being heard? Do you feel bitterness and resentment growing toward your partner? When was the last time you brought it to God in prayer and truly thanked God for your mate? Are you struggling to find quality time together? How about praying with your partner and asking God how he would like you to use your time?

As you begin to do these things, you'll notice that your focus automatically starts to shift away from you and your desires and over to God and your partner. As a result, communication problems begin to improve while anger and resentment fade away, resulting in a desire to spend more time together. If we will commit our relationship to God and make a conscious decision each day to put God and our partner first, our marriage will be full of happiness.

THE PROMISE OF JOY

The Bible never really promises us happiness, but it does promise us joy. There is a significant difference. It's easy to be happy when we have freedom from suffering, are financially secure and all our relationships are going well but if we have trouble with any of these, what happens to our happiness? It's probably gone. However, if we are in a right relationship with God and know we are safe in his hands, we still have joy.

Joy is not dependent on what happens to us. It is the peace that comes from knowing that God is in control of the details of life and the confidence that everything will be all right. Happiness is based upon circumstances, meaning if things go well, we are happy, but if it happens that something bad occurs our happiness is gone.

Before Jesus was crucified, he said "I have told you this so that my joy may be in you and that your joy may be complete" (John 15:11). "*Now is the time of your grief, but I will see you again and you will rejoice, and no one will take away your joy.*" (John 16:22). One of the fruits of the Spirit is joy (Gal 5:22). And, this joy doesn't leave in hard times. "*Consider it pure joy, my brothers and sisters, whenever you face trials of many kinds*" (James 1:2).

Most of our marriage has been filled with happiness. Losing our three babies did not bring happy times. However, even during those very dark days we never lost our joy—joy that came from the security and promises we have from resting in God's hands, and in knowing that one day we will be united with our babies.

Happiness is a great thing, if it is kept under God's control. Constant happiness does not exist in this life; because life has its hard times, and happiness and hard times don't mix well. But joy is a gift from God, and it can exist in all circumstances and situations.

Chapter Fifteen

PRACTICE PATIENCE

*"As a prisoner for the Lord, then, I urge
you to live a life worthy of the calling
you have received. Be completely humble
and gentle; be patient, bearing with
one another in love."*
—Ephesians 4:1-2

We are not finished products as individuals and as a couple, and we never will be. We are works in progress. It is important that we not lose sight of this fact. We need patience with ourselves and with each other. Do the following statements sound familiar?

"God, give me patience—right now!" Most of us have probably said some version of that prayer.

"He left the toilet seat up again."

"I'm waiting for my wife to finish dressing, and we're already twenty minutes late."

"I find—again—my husband's dirty socks and underwear on the floor instead of in the laundry basket."

"She is technologically challenged and wants me do something as simple as to load an app on her smart phone, which she should be able to do."

"I got so upset when I opened the dishwasher and saw that he had once again 'loaded the bowls the wrong way.'"

"I can't believe she left the gas tank in the car empty again."

Some behaviors and personal characteristics have been with us for a lifetime. Yes, these traits are annoying, but neither of us is likely to change very much. When two people with different personalities, preferences and quirks live together, they're bound to become irritated or angry at times. These things are real issues but being impatient is never going to make them get better.

THE POWER OF PATIENCE

Patience is the ability to deal with anything that doesn't work out the way we would like without reacting in anger or frustration. When couples who have been married for many years are asked their secret to marital success, many identify patience as one of the key ingredients. It's an essential virtue for living together day after day in relative peace, without constantly struggling to change our mate to our liking.

Patience in marriage begins with each of us growing in our own individual patience. The events of the day give us plenty of opportunity to practice our patience; waiting at the drive-through window, enduring rush hour traffic or doing our taxes. As we grow in patience outside the home, we bring the benefits home with us. Sometimes, the answer to the question "What have I done for my marriage today?" is "When I got caught in the traffic jam, I used it as a chance to pray and think rather than get frustrated."

Within marriage, patience involves discerning what needs to be changed and what needs to be tolerated. On our wedding day we probably consider our mate nearly perfect; before long we see a few things we could help them improve. Of course, we quickly find out that they don't necessarily want to be improved. In fact, they have a few ideas for our own improvement! We need to be patient with each other and learn to work together. Some behaviors need to be changed for the good of the marriage, and patience can help us to make the changes.

Patience does not mean that we do nothing when our mate is upset with us. It is not helpful to sit stone-faced and listen to their hurts and complaints and then get up and walk out of the room with no comment. This is not patience; it is selfishness and self-centeredness. Patience is caring enough to listen empathetically with a view of trying to understand what is being said and felt. Such listening requires time and is itself an expression of love.

Patience also means remaining calm when what the other

person is saying is hurtful. Patience says, "I care enough that no matter what you say or how you say it, I will listen and try to understand." When we become impatient, lose our temper and throw back cruel words to our partner, we come across as an enemy, not a friend. And they will likely fight the enemy or flee. So, it results in a big argument that no one wins; both of us walk away wounded and try to avoid each other for the next few days. All because of our impatience and selfishness.

On the other hand, had we been patient, we would have asked questions in an effort to understand. Once we understand the motivation behind the comments, we are more likely to have reasonable responses. We feel like friends, and friends responds positively to friends. The whole atmosphere remains positive because we chose to be patient.

In addition to being patient with each other, couples need to be patient with the marriage itself. Healthy marriages grow and change as we go through various stages, from honeymoon to empty nest and everything in between. Some stages hold excitement and promise, but others involve pain or boredom. These stages, although difficult, are normal. With patience, a couple can work through them and grow into the next stage with more love for and appreciation of each other. Like marriage itself, patience is the work of a lifetime. Each day brings opportunities to grow.

CONTROLLING IMPATIENCE

Patience opens doors to many good things, but impatience and its adult child, anger, build walls of hurt and alienation. One of the most difficult skills that partners must develop in a marriage is learning how to deal effectively with impatience and anger. Any time two people live together, there will be times when patience wears thin and tempers flare. When things don't go according to plan, our spouse doesn't act in the way we expect, or the kids are being crazy, impatience is a common response, and then often, anger.

It is very important to learn how to control our impatience before it turns to anger. We certainly have not been perfect, but here are a few practices that have helped us:

1. Understand what triggers impatience. There are many triggers like being too busy such as having enough rest, not feeling well, or not spending enough time together sexually. Understanding that you are impatient and understanding the cause of impatience is the first step to finding a solution.

2. Recognize when you start feeling impatient. There is usually some buildup, so learn to recognize when you are starting to feel impatient and take steps to calm down. Sometimes one of us will recognize impatience building in the other and will say something like, "Are we okay with each other?" or "Are you alright?"

3. Realize you aren't totally in control of your emotions or of the situation at those times of impatience. This is a big one. At the end of the day, impatience usually boils down to not having control in the way you believe you should, even subconsciously. If you can step outside of the moment, remind yourself that it's okay if things aren't going according to plan because plans do fail sometimes. Giving up an attempt to control circumstances will go a long way toward helping develop greater patience.

4. Apologize when you've been impatient. The emotional damage you created by losing your temper will not be removed just with the passing of time. However, if you acknowledge your impatience and ask your spouse for forgiveness, you are less likely to be impatient the next time.

5. Find a method to break the negative patterns of impatience. For some people, this means counting to ten before saying anything or taking a walk around the block before responding to your spouse.

6. Realize that impatience doesn't change the situation. A negative reaction will probably hurt others and embarrass you. More importantly, it doesn't demonstrate love.

THE DAMAGE OF ANGER

The famous American humorist Will Rogers once said, "People who fly into a rage always make a bad landing." It's hard to deal with an angry person and it's even harder when the angry person is your spouse. Anger—only one letter away from "danger" is poison to a marriage. The roots of anger can be recent or from years ago. They can stem from selfishness, self-hate, disappointment, unmet expectations, abuse, injustice, offenses real and perceived, jealousy, frustrated or unreachable dreams and goals, and many other sources. This is why finding the real root is so important. Anger creates a lot of damage to others; an angry person never just makes themselves miserable. Anger in a marriage and family can create feelings of bitterness, hostility, fear, resentment, revenge, and abandonment in other family members. And, on top of that, with people who struggle with anger, there is often a general self-awareness of the destructive effects, making them angrier at themselves which only intensifies the anger toward others. Anger is not usually solved overnight, but you should still urgently work to bring it under control.

If I (Al) could do one thing over in the years that our three girls we still growing up at home, it would be to control my impatience and anger that was frequently directed at our girls. I never yelled at them or struck them in anger, but I could humiliate them while trying to help them with their math and science homework. Understanding math and science has always been easy for me; that is why I have a PhD in Physics. When I tried to help the girls with math, and it did not come as easy to them, I would end up making them feel stupid. I have since apologized to them many times since they grew up, and we can all laugh about it now, but I wish I could go back and change the way I came across to them and made them feel. Just recently, I found a journal that our youngest daughter Keri had made as a part of her second-grade class assignment. We both had a good laugh as we looked through it. On the last page in bold letters we saw where she had written, "I HATE MATH!" While we thought it was funny, now as I think about it, I wonder whether that may have been her response to the pain that she saw me put her two older sisters through when she saw my impatience with them while I tried to help them with their math.

Some argue that God gets angry, Jesus got angry, and we are instructed to not sin in our anger (Ephesians 4:26). So, it must be alright to get angry sometimes, right? In our counseling, Gloria and I have seen enough damage done to couples by their anger that we believe that the best policy is to resolve never to take anger or irritation out on each other. Yes, Jesus got angry, but his anger was never about him, it was selfless. I am not sure that I have ever experienced selfless anger, mine always seems to be selfish.

So, we end this chapter just as we started it: *"be patient, bearing with one another in love."*

Chapter Sixteen

DON'T WORRY

"...do not worry about your life."
—Matthew 6:25

So many things in our life are totally out of our control. The unknown without a strong faith in God can produce fear and worry. We have already discussed the blessing of joy, but fear and worry can be major joy-stealers.

The summer before Al and me got married, Al worked as a Bible salesman in Dallas. My home was in Abilene, about a three-hour drive west from Dallas. On some weekends after he finished with his work, Al would drive to Abilene to see me. One of those weekends I was excitedly waiting for him to get there. It got later and later; I went to the window at every sound of a car. And with each trip to the window, I got more and more anxious. My mind went from one bad scene to the next. I envisioned a car wreck with Al thrown on the highway!

With that kind of imagination, I was the "wreck" emotionally by the time Al got there safe and sound. Remember, in the "old days" we didn't have cell phones, so it wasn't as easy as it is today to keep in close touch. After Al calmed me down, he went on to his friend's house, and I went to bed exhausted from needless fears and tears. The next morning, I replayed the night's scenario to my mom and dad. When I got to the frantic tears part, Daddy said, "Gloria, that is the craziest thing I've ever heard! If Al had been in an accident, you would have been in such a state that we would have to take care of you, and you would not be able to help Al. As it turned out, all your tears and worries were for nothing!" His words still ring in my ears as I remember that night. All my emotionalism did no good—only damage. I would like to say I have never worried since that time, but to my shame, there have been too many times when anxiety has controlled me.

Both that lesson and Daddy's own example have strengthened my convictions so that I have experienced more and more victories over worry. One of Daddy's favorite sayings that I have often quoted is "Worry is like a rocking chair—it gives you something to do, but it doesn't get you anywhere." At least a rocking chair can give some comfort; worry certainly does not! The apostle Paul in Philippians 4:6-7 gives us the antidote to worry: *"Do not be anxious about anything, but in everything, by prayer and petition, with thanksgiving, present your requests to God. And the peace of God, which transcends all understanding, will guard your hearts and your minds in Christ Jesus."* My dad was one of the most thankful persons I have ever known. Isn't it interesting that he was not a worrier? I am so grateful for a real-life display of the truth of this Biblical principle in the life of my dad. And I want to be the same example to my children and grandchildren.

A favorite quote about worry that we have used many times is by a French philosopher named Michel de Montaigne, who lived over five hundred years ago. He said, "My life has been filled with terrible misfortune; most of which never happened." We usually end up feeling foolish about whatever it was that made us anxious because most of the time the result is not nearly as bad as we imagined. There was a study conducted that showed that eighty-five percent of what was worried about never actually happened. And of the rest that did happen, nearly all the subjects discovered that either they could handle the difficulty better than originally expected, or the difficulty taught them a lesson worth learning.

Satan is a master at playing mind games with us. He tries to trick us into thinking that our worries are legitimate concerns. Certainly, we want to be concerned about the safety of our loved ones, our health or paying our bills. But there is a distinct difference between worry and concern. A worried person frets over the problem, and a concerned person prays and solves the problem.

In the New Testament the Greek word *merimnah* is often translated as "worry" and sometimes "anxiety" when it's used in the negative sense. This is the case when Jesus says, *"...do not worry about your life, what you will eat or drink; or about your body, what you will wear. Is not life more than food and the body more than clothes?"* (Matthew 6:25 NIV) However, when the same Greek word is used positively, it is often translated "concern". This is the case when Paul writes to the Philippians about Timothy's concern for them. *"I have no one else like him, who will show genuine concern for your welfare."* (Philippians 2:20 NIV) One major difference between these two uses of the word *merimnah* is the fact that genuine concern is always focused on others, but worry is not. In fact, worry is focused on self. When concern crosses over the line and becomes worry, it is no longer motivated by love, but by fear. So, what is the bottomline difference between worry and concern? It is how we position God in relationship to our problem. Shut him out of the loop, and we worry. But take the problem to God, believing that he has the power to solve it—that is concern.

Worry can rob our marriage of the joy that God intends for it to have. It can creep in and become a daily habit; money problems, sexual stress, petty arguments, job pressures...But, the real hooks are the bigger problems that inevitably will face us at some time in our marriage.

After we had lost three babies and were pregnant again, we had to fight Satan for the entire pregnancy with the worry that we might lose another baby. And years later, with the diagnosis of cancer, the temptation was to worry about what the future held for the two of us and how long we might have together. The answer, of course, is to surrender to God, and trust that he can and will take care of us.

God taught me (Gloria) a lesson years ago that has freed me in so many situations in which I am tempted to worry. As I was driving in stop-and-go traffic, I felt myself tensing up and getting more and more anxious. I was running late for an appointment, and there was nothing I could do to move any faster. The longer I sat there, the tighter my hands gripped the steering wheel—I was really uptight and worried about being late! Finally, I started praying, "LORD, you know where I need to be—help me to trust you to get me there." I took a deep breath, relaxed my tense shoulders and loosened my hands from the steering wheel. My open hands had my fingernail marks on them from my tight grip. It suddenly hit me that my being tense had accomplished nothing, but that praying and opening my hands had given me an instant peaceful feeling even in the midst of traffic. And then I remembered Psalms 88:9: *"I call to you, Lord, every day; I spread out my hands to you."*

That experience was the birth of my "open-hands prayer". Praying with open hands has become my expression in a physical way of trusting God and surrendering my will and my worries to him. This has become a common practice for me personally, but there are times when it is a real struggle for me to keep my hands open. I remember a walk on the beach when I was agonizing over a situation (interestingly, I can't remember the specific situation, but I do remember the battle I was feeling within). I was crying, praying and alternately opening my hands, then clenching my fists. I was fighting for control! Peace only comes when I open my hands and keep them open.

I often picture this struggle like a toddler clenching a piece of chocolate in his hands while his mother is telling him to give the candy to her. It is only a losing battle for the toddler. He can hold on to the chocolate until he ruins it by melting it in his hands. Then he also must deal with having to have his hands washed. No matter how hard he tries, his mother is stronger, and she can pry his little fingers away from the candy if she chooses. He may be missing an even better treat; his mom may have planned to give him his favorite dessert after his dinner! How much better it would have been for him if he had opened his hand, obeyed his mother and trusted her to give him what is best for him when it is best. By opening up our hands before God and giving him control of that problem, concern or whatever is in our hands, God then can leave it there, take it away, or replace it with something better. It is under his control. I have found my greatest peace when my hands are open!

It is so easy to get bogged down by worry. Worrying prevents us from living life fully, and from truly experiencing the richness of the marriage relationship. It is hard to hand-in-hand enjoy the pleasures of today when we are dwelling on the pains of the past or worrying about the what-ifs of the future. We cannot change the past, but we can ruin the present by worrying about the future. Let's learn from the past and plan for the future. The more we live in and enjoy the now, the more fulfilled we will be. God can take care of the rest.

Chapter Seventeen

GROW THROUGH THE HARD TIMES

"Consider it pure joy...whenever you face trials of many kinds, because you know that the testing of your faith produces perseverance. Let perseverance finish its work so that you may be mature and complete, not lacking anything."
—James 1:2-4

The real antidote to fear and worry is to have the faith that God can and will use the difficult things that come our way to shape us into what he wants us to be.

Traditional wedding vows go something like this: "I, Al, take you, Gloria, to be my wife. I promise to be true to you in good times and in bad, in sickness and in health. I will love and honor you all the days of my life." Almost all of us make those vows without realizing that our lives together are not going to be all good times; some bad times are going to inevitably be mixed in with the good. The wedding cards talk about "happily ever after." The wedding songs sing about "happily ever after." Every girl has seen the movies and read the books about the handsome prince sweeping away his beautiful princess and their living "happily ever after." Most of us identify marriage with this magical theme, and search for our dream partner, so we can get married and live "happily ever after." This is exciting, it's heartwarming, but quite far from reality.

Marriage requires lots of hard work, and there will be hard times. It is unfortunate that these hard times aren't talked about more as part of preparation for marriage. After all, anyone who is happily married will agree that they have had to endure some really difficult situations themselves. Difficult hardships are part of all marriages. Our inability to anticipate the bad events and to talk about them prior to their happening really hurts many couples when they are going through them. It is also the unexpectedness of bad times that causes some couples to panic and mention the word "divorce." Couples cannot anticipate the coming of bad times in their marriage as they walk down the aisle, because they cannot imagine anything other than the love they are feeling at the time. But, if we will willingly accept struggles as being a necessary part of personal as well as relationship growth, then we can look forward to whatever God wants us to learn from those times.

Al and I were just such a couple, deeply in love and on top of the world. We were struggling college students writing the perfect script for our happy lives. After a year of marriage, I got pregnant (oops!) The pregnancy went well until I went into labor seven weeks early. Our baby boy only lived three days. What a shock it was and how much it hurt. He would have been the first grandbaby on both sides of our family and suddenly everything was different. I remember realizing how vulnerable we were— bad things could happen to us. We had to face something we did not like and did not understand. Our faith was tested like never before.

After this loss we had a sense that surely we had suffered our share of hardships. However, pain and hardships do not come in "fair" doses by our definition and understanding. After we had a healthy baby girl, I got pregnant again; this time with twin girls. They were also born early, as was our son, and only lived one day. How could this be happening again? We were crushed. What do you do with hardship or with painful situations? We just want the pain to go away. We try to explain it or understand it or even deny it. We questioned God, begging to understand. We remember asking, "Did we do something wrong? Are you punishing us? Why is this happening to us?" There are so many things that happen to us or around us that we cannot understand or explain.

A friend recently agonized over the sudden death of her thirty-two-year-old husband and being left as a widow with three young children. Who of us would not be asking, "Why?" Humanly, we look for answers, and not infrequently, the answers we seek don't come.

For us as Christians, we know that our God is all powerful, but we also know that Satan is a very real and powerful enemy. We often have struggled with trying to decide if a particular situation was from God or from Satan. We have come to understand that God and Satan often use the same circumstances, and it is up to us individually to choose which direction we will go in any given situation. We can pull closer to God, become more dependent on his word and each other, or pull away from him and convince ourselves that he doesn't really care about us.

It is always God's will to pull us closer to him; it is always Satan's will to pull us away from God! It is our choice which way we go. Years ago, I (Gloria) heard it said, "You can waste your time, your energy, your money, but don't waste your suffering!" This statement got my attention. It is frightening to think that I might prolong or repeat painful experiences by failing to learn from them. During the pain of losing our babies, I could sense a difference between asking "why?" and demanding "why?" The demanding attitude—the "tell me or else" quickly leads to bitterness, which pulls us away from God. The asking "why?" was a soul-wrenching cry for an answer, yet a willing surrender to a loving God whether or not the answer came.

Surrender brings comfort and peace and reinforces our trust in God. As we trust him, we begin to learn some of life's greatest lessons, even in our pain. As we look back at our life together, it seems that the deepest lessons we have learned and the greatest character changes we have made have come through the hard times. Whatever happens in life, we want to draw closer to God knowing he gives us the ultimate victory. We don't want us to waste our suffering!

Hard times can take many forms such as illness and loss of loved ones, infidelity, addiction, job loss, infertility, miscarriage, in-law problems, finances, and challenging children. We have observed that severe hardship and heartbreak will either draw you together or drive you apart but will never leave you the same. It often will intensify the kind of relationship that you have before hardship comes. A close, healthy relationship will generally grow stronger in a crisis; a weak one will often crumble. Our losing our babies, losing our parents, and six years ago my contracting cancer drove us to our knees, but each dark chapter resulted in our growing stronger spiritually and growing closer to each other.

On the other hand, a couple that we knew suffered the

tragedy of their young daughter drowning in a back-yard pool. This couple did not have a strong marriage; and rather than growing closer, tragically they divorced.

Here are a few things that have helped us in our hard times:

1. **Believe God will keep his promises;** the promise to never give us more than we can handle (1 Corinthians 10:13), to work out everything for good (Romans 8:28), that God will comfort us in all of our troubles (2 Corinthians 1:3-4) and God will use hard times to help us grow (Romans 5:3-18).

2. **Pray together every day.** We have discovered that often while listening to the other one pray, we learn so much about what each other is feeling and thinking. It also reminds us that God is the one who will carry us through...together! We have done this for fifty-six years and call this the spiritual glue of our marriage.

3. **Communicate everything together.** Remember that you are a team and that no team works well without good communication. Men and women process hardship differently. The way that I mourned over the loss of my mother was very different and more verbal than the way that Al grieved over the loss of his mother. Neither was the right or wrong way to grieve, but our communication was important in our being able to understand, help and support each other in our loss.

4. **A regular sexual relationship is crucial.** Often, we just don't feel like it, but the physical closeness is very important in helping us to feel totally united.

5. **Keep your sense of humor.** Even on the hard days, find reasons to laugh together. You can't always control your circumstances, but you can always choose how you respond.

6. **Never give up!** Don't expect problems to be solved automatically. Time doesn't necessarily heal all things. Work together to find solutions. Resolve together that you're going to keep going "for better or for worse." Your commitment will make all the difference!

> 7. **Surround yourself with advisors.** You need friends who love both of you, who are wise, who have time for you and who will not be afraid to tell you what you need to hear. Friends who will not give up on you, but who will be "wind beneath your wings!"

Looking back over the years, we can see God's molding and shaping of our character through the hardest of times. Only God knows what kind of people we would be and what kind of marriage we would have if we had not experienced loss. And we are amazed at the opportunities we have to help and *"comfort those in any trouble with the comfort we ourselves have received from God"* (2 Corinthians 1:4).

None of us enjoy hard times, but they are a part of God's plan for growing and maturing us as individuals and as a couple. May we let God use them to shape us into the couple that he desires for us to be—one made in his image.

Chapter Eighteen

ENJOY ROMANCE

*"How beautiful and how delightful you
are, my love, with all your charms!"*
—Song of Songs 7:6

A significant part of the foundation of any marriage is a solid commitment of unconditional love. One of the great joys of life is romance. Romance is an outward expression of that love, the language of the heart; it is the sense that you're still being pursued, that you are uniquely special. Not surprisingly, men and woman can have very different definitions of romance. When asked to describe the purpose of romance, a woman may use words such as friendship, relationship, endearment, and tenderness. For them, romance may involve love songs, flowers, chick flicks, candle-light dinners, long walks on the beach; things that evoke heart throbbing feelings.

Ask a man the same question, and most will answer with one of the shortest words in the English language—sex. For him, physical oneness and affirmation of his manhood equal romance. The guy is thinking, "If romance is about feeling emotionally connected, and sex is my way of being emotionally connected, and we're already being romantic, then why not now?" Women typically go from romance to sex, and men go from sex to romance, and men don't understand what the big deal is. But it is not just a big deal; it is a huge deal.

NOTICE TO MEN: Romance is not sex, it is not a way to get sex, it is not foreplay. This is very difficult for most men to understand and accept, because many of the things involved in romance just naturally trigger our sex drive. We both often humorously quote Raymond in "Everybody Loves Raymond" responding to Debra's desire for cuddling with "and that leads to 'lower cuddling!'" We don't understand that those same things don't trigger the same sex drive in most women. Men and women really are different!

Without the kind of romance that we are discussing, sex can seem contrived and selfish to the wife, feeling her husband just sees her as sex object. He may wonder why she is so passive in bed, while she wonders why he is so selfish. This can lead to resentment and bitterness on both of their parts. When a marriage is struggling sexually, often it is missing the kind of romance that the wife craves. We mentioned in Chapter 5 on respect, that men typically need more emphasis on respect and women need more emphasis on love. Romance is a huge part of love that women need.

When we were dating, all we could think about was how exciting and romantic it was to be together. Back then, we couldn't do enough to please each other. But as time passed, life happened, the kids came, we got accustomed to married life and stopped making those special efforts for each other. Most of us run at the speed of light and wake up one day and realize, "I don't feel very close to my mate anymore." The truth is that it happens to the best of us. We need to make romance a part of our everyday diet in our marriage relationship with the emphasis being on meeting our mates' romantic needs, not just our own. This means becoming a student of your spouse and learning what pleases him or her. The men will naturally focus on physical intimacy: "Dress up in a sexy negligee," or "Meet me at the front door without any clothes." The women, however, will want things like "Take me to a romantic, candle-lit restaurant," "Spend time talking with me," or "Sit in front of a fire and cuddle." Meeting your spouse's romantic needs means remembering what pleases him or her and sacrificing your own needs to meet those of your mate. Selfishness and romance do not mix well.

Let's look at what we call the big three of romance: Attention, Appreciation and Affection.

ATTENTION

A major key to romance is our thinking. When we were dating, no one had to tell us to think romantically about each other. Before we married, we were drawn to the affection that Gloria's parents showed for one another, and we decided that was going to be the way we would be. Easier said than done. Only after we made a firm commitment to making that a high priority in our marriage did it happen. It was not just a one-and-done commitment, but a daily commitment.

Not thinking about being romantic will allow the romance to slowly die, but negative, critical thinking will sabotage and kill it. Paul urges us in 2 Corinthians 10:5 to "*take captive every thought to make it obedient to Christ.*" Resolving conflict and replacing negating thoughts with positive, loving ones is essential to sustaining a romantic marriage.

Put effort into taking care of yourself; take time to look, feel and smell good. Yes, things start to sag with time, but we don't have to accelerate the process! Exercise and healthy diet do more than just make the doctor happy.

The wife needs to feel safe and secure with her man. That happens when her husband is leading her spiritually, and she sees that God is his top priority. But she also needs to feel that he will try to provide for her needs and keep her safe physically. One of the times that I saw Gloria very hurt and angry was near midnight one night after an appointment. I needed the car to pick up someone at the airport, and she needed to go home. I saw no reason why she couldn't just take the bus home. She let me know calmly, but sternly, that a husband is to protect his wife, and she didn't feel protected or safe. Lesson learned; I didn't make that mistake again.

Regular time alone together is essential, not just in the bedroom. Some studies have shown that the typical couple spends only four minutes a day in meaningful conversation with each other. Go out at least a few hours each week. It doesn't have to be an expensive date for you to be alone together; use some imagination, like you did when dating. Dream together, talk about what feeds your romantic needs, laugh, cry, encourage each other. Go for a walk, movie, or ballgame. Meet for lunch. Take a dance class together. Also, get away overnight as often as possible, at least every couple of months.

Create memories together. One day in Boston, we had a beautiful snowstorm. Al called me from work and said, "Come meet me at the Old North Bridge in Concord and let's take a walk in the snow." I met Al there, and it was perfect, like a scene out of a movie. No one was there but us and no one else had walked through the snow. We strolled for an hour hand in hand in six inches of snow. That was many years ago, but both of us still treasure that time together and often revisit it in our memory as one of our special times together.

APPRECIATION

We need to communicate in as many ways as we can, "You are really on my heart" and "You're very important to me". Focusing on anything you can do, as creatively as you can to make your spouse feel cherished and valued.

Tell each other what you appreciate about them every day. Try this: make a list of twenty-five of your mate's most desirable traits and read the list daily to yourself, thinking of and thanking God for your spouse and then express appreciation to your mate for one of those traits every day.

Husbands; tell her she is beautiful (beauty is more than skin deep). Women who hear their husband tell them they're beautiful become more beautiful. Men who tell their wives they're beautiful believe it with more conviction every time the words leave their lips. It's a win-win.

Complement each other in front of others. And don't correct each other in front others—including the kids.

AFFECTION

There is great power in tender touch. Wives often complain that their husbands touch them only when they want sex. Most women like hand holding, kissing, and gentle physical closeness more than men do. There is a saying by Virginia Satir, a respected family therapist, "We need four hugs a day for survival. We need eight hugs a day for maintenance. We need twelve hugs a day for growth."[1]

So, guys, don't wait for bedtime to touch your wife. Make it part of the way you communicate every day. And be a gentleman; gentlemen are courteous, respectful, well-mannered, generous, and charming. Stand up when she leaves the table, open the car door, walk on the street side of the sidewalk, help her on with her jacket, run to the car for her umbrella... you get the picture. Understand that little things mean a lot; bringing her one rose, probably has the same impact as bring her a dozen roses.

Gloria and I from the very start of our marriage decided to

kiss after every meal, to hold hands at every opportunity and to kiss "hello" and "goodbye." We tell each other many times a day that we love each other, and we love "love notes" and cards. The power of a love note was made apparent one day in Boston. We had shared an unusually special time of making love that morning. Both of us had appointments at the same place later that day, but at different times. As I drove into the parking lot. I saw her car. I quickly tore a page out of my small spiral notebook and wrote on it, "You are the best!" That one simple note became a treasure to Gloria, and she still has it in her Bible more than thirty years later!

So, what kind of marriage do you want? With or without romance? Do you want to live with weeds or roses? Ho hum, day in day out sameness? Or exciting, vibrant, growing, passionate? The two of you can choose—you can change and you can make the difference.

END NOTES

1. Marcus Felicetti, "10 Reasons Why We Need at Least 8 Hugs a Day" https://www.mindbodygreen.com/0-5756/10-Reasons-Why-We-Need-at-Least-8-Hugs-a-Day.html.

Chapter Nineteen

BUILD SEXUAL INTIMACY

"Strengthen me with raisins,
refresh me with apples,
for I am faint with love.
His left arm is under my head,
and his right arm embraces me."
—Song of Songs 2:5-6

Coming together sexually is a tremendously important part of marriage; the touches, tastes, smells, sounds, sights, movements and feelings. All the inhibitions and barriers come down, and we invite each other into our most private spaces. There is a reason it is called "making love." It is our most meaningful way to express love for each other. Of all our relationship needs, sex is the only one that cannot be met by anyone else, only each other. Genesis 2:24 says: *"For this reason a man will leave his father and mother and be united to his wife, and they will become one flesh."* When the writer said the man and woman become "one flesh," he was talking about sex.

Let us say at the outset that some may have serious health challenges that make the sexual relationship difficult. Even then it is often still possible to satisfy each other sexually in other ways than intercourse.

'Sex' and 'intimacy' are often used interchangeably, but they are distinctly different. Sex is simply the act of intercourse; the physical gratification of enjoying a good sexual experience and orgasm with your partner. The sexual act can happen with or without intimacy and still be great; but with intimacy added, the results are incredible. Intimacy is not physical but is something much deeper. In fact, there are several types of intimacy, but there are two that are important in our discussion of marriage: emotional and sexual intimacy. In order to achieve true sexual intimacy, there must first be emotional intimacy.

EMOTIONAL INTIMACY

Most of us want to love and be loved, to feel safe in a relationship, to be known and accepted for who we really are when all our masks are removed and we are free to share all our dreams and our failings. That's what emotional intimacy is all about. By achieving that level of intimacy, we can share our deepest feelings, joys, fears, secrets, desires, failings and frustrations while knowing we are heard, embraced and admired. Moreover, it involves not only being known and accepted in these ways, but also providing the same for your partner.

SEXUAL INTIMACY

Having sexual intimacy means that you and your partner share a special unique physical bond that is intensified by an emotional bond. You understand each other on a sexual level that has emotion behind it, instead of it just being a physical act. Being intimate with your partner requires you to be open and honest with him or her, and it is from this state of intimacy that great sex happens. The physical act takes on a new dimension in which you are not only one physically, but also emotionally and this is almost like looking into each other's soul. It allows you both to be totally vulnerable with each other as you touch and pleasure each other. The results quite often are "skyrockets in flight."

We need to work to make our sex together a continuing process of discovery and mutual enjoyment. No matter how many times we have made love to each other, the wonder and awe of mutual attraction and fulfillment can still be there. Our sex life does not have to become boring in a long-term marriage. We can honestly say that, while we don't have nearly as much stamina as we did in our twenties, our love making in our late seventies is the most special and satisfying that it has ever been. As the years go by, we still work to make it better and better. We both know each other so well by now; what makes each other feel good, our likes, dislikes, habits and so on. But we also know that life can get in the way. Careers, kids, finances, health, and many other things can hinder sexual intimacy. These everyday things can interfere with both our desire, energy, and time to put into our sex life, so we need to work to keep it high on our priority list.

SOME KEYS TO A GOOD SEXUAL RELATIONSHIP

Here are some things that have helped us:

1. A unified walk together with God. God created us to give pleasure to each other in a committed marriage relationship, but only when both of us are following his plan for our lives. Secular studies show that those of us who are most surrendered to God have the best sex lives.

2. Appreciating the differences between men and women. Men often view sex as a physical release and a way to reconnect with their wives, while women tend to see it as an outgrowth of their emotional intimacy. Gary Chapman in his book *The Five Love Languages*[1] writes, "Most sexual problems in marriage have little to do with physical technique but everything to do with meeting emotional needs." He gives more details to help understand some of the basic differences between men and women: For men, sexual desire is physically based. That is, the desire for sexual intercourse is stimulated by the buildup of sperm cells which creates a physical push for release. Thus, a man's desire for sexual intercourse has a physical root.

3. For the woman, sexual desire is rooted in her emotions, not her physiology. There is nothing physically that builds up and pushes her to have intercourse. Her desire is emotionally based. If she feels loved, admired and appreciated by her husband (See Chapter 18 on romance), then she has a desire to be physically intimate with him. Early in our marriage Al and I realized that our sex drives were different, as we learned is the case with most couples. Most often it is the man who has the greater drive, but sometimes it is the woman. There were times when I thought that sex was all Al thought about, there were times when I thought there was something wrong with me, and there were times when I thought everything was perfect. We have often wondered why God made men and women so different. Wouldn't it have been easier and more pleasurable if

we had the same needs level? These differences are designed by God to show us how to give ourselves to each other in love. According to the Bible, true love can be expressed only through unselfishness. Were it possible for me to love my husband while pursuing my own selfish desires, I would never know the beauty of real love. A great sex life is only possible as both the husband and wife commit to laying their needs down for the other. Marriage exposes our selfishness like no other relationship. If we hold on to a selfish concern for meeting our own needs rather than being sure we are meeting each other's needs, there will be problems. Paul gives this godly perspective in 1 Corinthians 7:3-5: "The husband should fulfill his marital duty to his wife, and likewise the wife to her husband. The wife's body does not belong to her alone but also to her husband. In the same way, the husband's body does not belong to him alone but also to his wife. Do not deprive each other except by mutual consent and for a time, so that you may devote yourselves to prayer. Then come together again so that Satan will not tempt you because of your lack of self-control." God has given husbands and wives the unique privilege and responsibility of fulfilling each other's sexual needs. I came to realize that though Al has the stronger sex drive, I need our sexual relationship as much as he does. While I appreciate and enjoy the physical satisfaction, I primarily need the emotional closeness and what it does for our relationship.

4. Learn how to please each other. Not only are men and women different, each person is different. A great part of sexual intimacy is learning how to pleasure each other. I learned many years ago that there were two four-letter words that Al doesn't like to hear during our love making: "don't" and "stop", unless they are used together! We all come in various sizes, shapes and sensitivities. While the woman may not have as large a sex drive as her husband, her capacity for intense sexual

pleasure can at least match his, because God created the woman, not the man, with the only organ in either one that is solely intended to give sexual pleasure: the clitoris. And while it is much smaller than the penis, it has twice as many nerve endings. There is so much to learn about making love to each other and so much fun doing it!

5. Enjoy the togetherness without specific goals. While orgasm is certainly important, there is much more to sexual intimacy. For many women achieving an orgasm is difficult. In fact, recent studies show that less than one woman in five can orgasm by intercourse alone,[2] most women will need some manual or oral stimulation. If sex becomes so goal oriented, undue pressure can be put on both the husband and the wife. Early in our marriage, not knowing this, I was determined that Gloria was going to orgasm every time during intercourse (that was before we discovered oral sex), and we would both end up frustrated. It was sad to focus so much on the "destination" that we failed to enjoy the "journey." Although orgasm is not the only goal of lovemaking, it is still a very pleasurable culmination. It is especially vital for the wife to realize how important it is to her husband to be able to bring her to completion in an orgasm. A large part of his fulfillment, sometimes even the most important part, as a husband and lover is to fulfil his wife. The husband also needs to realize that his wife may not need an orgasm as frequently as he does, and that satisfying him in a "quickie" at times can also fulfill her.

While the husband is normally the "pursuer" and initiator, a man desperately wants to be wanted by his wife and thrills to her being the one to initiate regularly. Share with one another your sexual desires. Be open and honest about what you want and teach each other what pleases you and how to achieve it. Be open to trying new things.

Every time of making love is not going to be perfect. Some may be disappointments. But most will be really good; others will be great. Some will be memory-making, amazing true sexual intimacy. All those times of love provide the glue that hold us together as one. We smile and thank God for giving us each other, sex, sexual intimacy and a lifetime of great memories.

END NOTES

1. Gary Chapman, *The Five Love Languages* (Zondervan, 1995).
2. Debby Herbenick et al., "Women's Experiences With Genital Touching, Sexual Pleasure, and Orgasm: Results From a U.S. Probability Sample of Women Ages 18 to 94" August 9, 2017, https://www.tandfonline.com/doi/full/10.1080/0092623X.2017.1346530.

Chapter Twenty

AVOID PORN LIKE THE PLAGUE

"Put to death, therefore, whatever belongs to your earthly nature: sexual immorality, impurity, lust, evil desires and greed, which is idolatry."
—Colossians 3:5

Sexual intimacy is one of God's great gifts to a married couple. Porn is one of Satan's great curses; he uses it to destroy the sexual intimacy and even the marriage.

The year 1953 marked the beginning of a major attack by Satan on sexual morality and marriage. That was the year that Hugh Hefner published the first copy of Playboy. Before then pornography was pretty much considered slutty. Hefner helped transform it into big business as a harmless pleasure enjoyed by respectable and successful people.

And then came the Internet, which changed everything.

Once porn hit the Web in the 1990s, suddenly there was nothing but a few clicks between anyone with an Internet connection and the most graphic, raunchiest and most sexually explicit material in the world. By 2004, porn sites were getting three times more visitors than Google, Yahoo!, and MSN Search combined. Men who would never have dared to enter an adult book store can now watch porn on their cell phones. And today it is not just men; more than one in three women watch porn at least once a week. Even more alarming in the United States is the trend of the younger population: Shockingly, women in the 18-24 demographic watched more porn than men 18-24 by a whopping five percent.[1] The statistics of those claiming to be Christian is nearly as alarming. Several Christian counselors has expressed his opinion that pornography is now the greatest threat to Christianity today!

The effects of porn on marriage are widespread and devastating. One researcher, after completing a major study of pornography, called it a "quiet family killer." His study found that fifty-six percent of divorces had one partner with an obsessive interest in porn.[2] Great marital sex involves more than technique, stamina, or experience. The genuine passion built up between two people in love connecting in the highest physical form of intimacy is what makes for great sex. This is difficult to achieve even without porn introduced into the equation. Children, stress, and busyness all take their toll on genuine passion. Pornography will destroy it. In studies, many women will say they don't feel that their porn-addicted husband is truly present when they make love.

I (Al) am writing this chapter, so it is written from a man's perspective. It is estimated that at least ninety percent of American men have watched porn on the Internet; but the number of women viewers is growing rapidly. One group set up a study focused on the views of men who had never watched porn, and they could find no one who had never watched porn![3] Until recently, pornography has primarily been a man's struggle, and most studies have been done about the short and long term effects of men's use of porn. We assume that similar damage is being done to the woman and her marriage because of her use, but not enough time has passed for good studies to have been performed. So, let's examine in the following paragraphs some of the reasons that a man's use of pornography in marriage is so destructive.

Porn breaks trust. While I have never watched porn regularly, I have struggled with it on several occasions in our marriage. Enough so that I asked Gloria to ask me from time to time if I had been tempted to watch it. One time when she asked me, I said "no." A day later she walked in my office and caught me watching a porn site. Understandably, she was deeply hurt and very angry. She said, "I can and will forgive you for watching, and even for lying to me; but how can I trust you anymore to tell me the truth?" We did work through it, and I did regain her trust but we both remember that as the hardest time ever in our relationship. (I made great effort to regain her trust, including putting porn blocks on all our computers and phones with her having the only password.)

Most porn use in a marriage is kept hidden; it requires darkness and secrecy to maintain its power over us. When a husband and wife hide things (other than fun surprises), it's living a lie. We can break this stranglehold and expose our sin to the light. Ephesians 5:13-14 exhorts, *"But when anything is exposed by the light, it becomes visible, for anything that becomes visible is light. Therefore it says, 'Awake, O sleeper, and arise from the dead, and Christ will shine on you.'"*

Porn destroys self-esteem. When a husband watches porn and his wife discovers it, she immediately thinks something is wrong with her. Women spend a lot of time beating themselves up and obsessing about their faults. A husband's porn use validates all the negative things his wife thinks about herself. If she only looked different, lost weight, was blonde, had larger breasts, was sexy, wore better clothes, or fit into the right size—these are all things that flood her brain, and more importantly, her heart. Ultimately, she starts to believe she is not enough and has failed her husband sexually. It is obvious to her that if her husband did not have unfulfilled desires, he would not have turned to porn.

Porn creates destructive comparisons and unreal expectations. When we fill our minds with the false images of porn, we take those expectations with us to the bedroom. This leads to disappointment for the husband. Studies show that porn makes viewers more critical of their partner and less satisfied with their romantic relationship and sex life. In porn, finding a "partner" is effortless. She is always ready, willing, and longing for our attention. This partner has nothing else to do with her time but wait for us, breathless and perpetually aroused. She is young, attractive, sexually adventurous, and anxious to please. She will never get bored or annoyed, never have an "off" day. In fact, all she will ever want is wild, ecstatic orgasms that look real! And if this porn-partner ever fails to keep us entertained, she can simply be exchanged with the click of a computer mouse. Porn promises rapture. It is probably wilder than anything we as a couple have been able to create in our bedroom. How can our wife compete with that?

Porn is selfish, self-centered and self-serving. Viewing porn doesn't require that husbands be lovers of their wives. In the counterfeit world of porn, sex simply involves an image or video, masturbation and orgasm. The sexual arousal is immediate, and gratification is instant; it's all about personal pleasure. And the variety is stimulating. Men, who can ejaculate in about two minutes with the right images have endless access to fast sex every day—and any time of day. Porn places the focus on self, not on intimacy.

Porn alters the brain chemistry and can quickly become addictive. (The following paragraph is adapted from an eye-opening website www.fightthenewdrug.org).

It may be surprising, but porn use affects the brain in ways very similar to addictive drugs and can be just as addictive. Deep inside the brain, there's something called a "reward center" which releases "pleasure" chemicals into our brain whenever we do something healthy, like enjoy a romantic time together. The "high" we get from that chemical rush makes us want to repeat that behavior again and again. When porn or addictive substances are used, they give the brain a "false signal." Since the brain can't tell the difference between the porn and a real, healthy reward, it goes ahead and activates the reward center, which makes the brain start developing a craving for the fake reward. With frequent use, the cravings get stronger, and the user is motivated to use more and more.

Researchers have found that Internet porn and addictive substances have very similar effects on the brain, and they are significantly different from how the brain reacts to healthy, natural pleasures like sex. When we're enjoying a romantic encounter, eventually our cravings will drop, and we'll feel satisfied. Why? Because our brain has a built-in "off" switch for natural pleasures. But Porn, like addictive drugs, goes right on increasing the craving without giving the brain a break. Over time, excessive levels of "pleasure" chemicals cause the porn consumer's brain to develop tolerance, just like the brain of a drug user.

Frequent porn users will end up turning to porn more often or seeking out more extreme versions, or both, to feel excited again. And once the porn habit is established, quitting can even lead to withdrawal symptoms similar to drugs. And tragically, often they find that they can no longer respond sexually to their real mates, though they can still function with porn. They would rather masturbate to porn than have sex with their wife. In fact, in a recent brain scan study, about sixty percent of compulsive porn users reported erectile dysfunction, leading to major problems in the bedroom.

Pornography, whether used infrequently or as an addiction, is a big deal. And it can have a major negative impact on our marriages. God intends for there to only be two of us in the bedroom when we are making love. When we use porn, our mind doesn't forget what we saw and heard. It is nearly impossible to not fantasize about those porn scenes while loving one another. That is not only a sin before God, but it cheapens and degrades our love making and prevents the two of us from truly being one. The good news is that we can overcome the ongoing use of pornography and the damage it has done. Make a real commitment to God to be done with it forever; and if you continually fail to keep that commitment, get help, either from a strong Christian or a dedicated support group. It takes time and prayer to erase those graphic memories, but they will eventually fade away. Satan wants to ruin one of God's greatest gifts to a married couple, but God will help us overcome if we do it his way.

END NOTES _____

1. Amanda de Cadenet, "Survey Finds More Than 1 In 3 Women Watch Porn At Least Once A Week", July 26, 2017, https://fightthenewdrug.org/survey-finds-one-in-three-women-watch-porn-at-least-once-a-week/.

2. Kevin B Skinner, "Is Porn Really Destroying 500,000 Marriages Annually?", December 12, 2011, https://www.psychologytoday.com/us/blog/inside-porn-addiction/201112/is-porn-really-destroying-500000-marriages-annually.

3. Jonathan Liew, "All men watch porn, scientists find", December 2, 2009, https://www.telegraph.co.uk/women/sex/6709646/All-men-watch-porn-scientists-find.html.

Chapter Twenty-One

FIND ADVENTURE AND MAKE MEMORIES

"Enjoy life with your wife, whom you love..."
—Ecclesiastes 9:9

Memory is one of God's great gifts, and he often called his people to use it as a reminder of his goodness and power. When the Israelites crossed the Jordan River into the Promised Land, he said, "*Go over before the ark of the Lord your God into the middle of the Jordan. Each of you is to take up a stone on his shoulder, according to the number of the tribes of the Israelites, to serve as a sign among you. In the future, when your children ask you, 'What do these stones mean?' tell them that the flow of the Jordan was cut off before the ark of the covenant of the LORD. When it crossed the Jordan, the waters of the Jordan were cut off. These stones are to be a memorial to the people of Israel forever*" (Joshua 4:5-7). And we take communion each week based on this verse, among other Bible scriptures, "And he took bread, gave thanks and broke it, and gave it to them, saying, "*This is my body given for you; do this in remembrance of me*" (Luke 22:19). The word "remember" is used over two hundred and fifty times in the Bible, so remembering must be pretty important.

Imagine what marriage would be like if we could not remember anything that happened last year, or last week, yesterday or even five minutes ago. No memory of the great time in the bedroom last night, no memory of a fantastic cruise together last year, no recollection of the beautiful sunset that you enjoyed hand-in-hand, no memory of sharing your favorite meal together, no memory of the last "I love you"...well, you get the idea. A marriage is built on shared memories over the years. We make memories so we have something to look back on, no matter how old we get.

In this chapter we want to talk, not just about memory, but the importance of creating special memories together. Do you know what can kill love in marriage as fast as anything else? Boredom. After the wedding bells, life happens; and the sense of excitement often lessens. And when children come along, it can take all our energy just to keep the family functioning. Life can start to seem routine and even overwhelming. God never intended for our marriage to be boring! When we get bored with each other, it's all too easy to start ignoring each other's needs, and to stop feeling that special feeling about each other. How often does the whole evening go by watching our favorite TV show or movie or playing video games? It may seem fun at the time, but if you try to remember some great, fun event ten years ago, we guarantee you that it didn't involve television or computers or games. It had to do with something you were doing together. Making memories means you have to be doing something that is memorable!

Helen Keller said, "Life is either a daring adventure or nothing at all." Marriage should be an incredible, thrilling, astounding, life-long adventure; God designed it that way. Adventure is the perfect solution for boredom and for creating memories. What do we mean by "adventure?" A dictionary definition is "an action involving unknown danger or risks" or "an exciting or unusual experience." Certainly, we are not advocating that you attempt going over Niagara Falls in a barrel, climb Mount Everest or attempt some other life-threatening feat. But, experiencing unusual activities together that have some built in excitement and a safe degree of risk can help keep marriage fresh and alive.

From the very start of our marriage, we had a goal to never let things become dull and ordinary. Creating adventures that make memories takes dedication and creativity. Here are some ways that kept marriage exciting for us and produced special memories:

- SURPRISES—One of the first things to go in a long-term relationship is the element of surprise. It is so easy to get into a routine and stop thinking creatively. Nothing adds adventure to life like the unexpected; a surprise goes a long way. And these surprises don't have to be expensive. Usually the more creative gifts or experiences, ones with a personal touch, are the best. A love note in his briefcase or in her iPad cover, a late-night candlelight dinner at home after the kids are in bed, one of you orchestrating a surprise overnight together, etc. I still get excited when I remember a night decades ago when we were driving home from an appointment. Gloria told me to follow her direction, and she took me to a local hotel room that she had booked for the night. She had packed a bag, and we had a night together that I will never forget! Planning surprises can initiate those weak-in-the-knees passionate feelings that you felt in the earlier stage of your relationship.

- **SPECIAL TIMES**—Do new things with each other once a year, once a month, once a week. Make it fun experiencing new things together. The same endorphins that were flying on your honeymoon will continue to help make memories whenever you do an exciting new thing. We took turns planning our weekly date, where each date needed to be new and creative; it's no fair just choosing to go to a movie and out to eat. A simple Internet search of your community calendars will give you lots of great ideas.

- **CREATE A BUCKET LIST TOGETHER**—Making a bucket list of the things the two of you want to experience together will create added excitement and closeness in your marriage, plus it will give you fun goals to shoot for. We had always wanted to take a ride in a hot air balloon, so we went on New Year's Day of the new millennium, 2000. We have swum with sharks in the South Pacific. We have parasailed in the Red Sea. Let your mind go wild.

- **SEX**—Spice up your sex life. Talk openly about what specific ways you'd like to make sex more exciting. Try something that is a bit daring for you, but never pressure your mate to do something that makes him or her uncomfortable; be sure to respect each other's opinions and reach a mutual agreement about how to make your sex life more adventurous. Sadly, adventure in the bedroom is one of the first things that can 'slide' when you have children and responsibilities grow.

- **GET-AWAYS & SPECIAL TRIPS**—Spend 24-hours away from home together frequently. When we think about adventures, we often think big vacations or long trips, but getting away as a couple locally can be more realistic and be just as adventurous. Make every fifth anniversary special and the tenth one extra special. Save up the money for it and plan it far enough in advance that you have months or years to get excited about it.

- **CHOOSE AN ADVENTURE OUT OF YOUR COMFORT ZONE** —Scary experiences bond hearts. The exhilaration of stepping outside your comfort zone and learning or doing something new spices up life. Find a zip-line or rock-climbing wall and schedule a date. Learn to golf, paddle board or ski. Take a cooking or dance class together. I sky dived with my daughter Keri on her fortieth birthday, while Gloria kept her fingers crossed and prayed—once was enough, but it was an adventure for us all!

- **GOD'S WORK**—No amount of our planning for adventure can come close to the results produced when God intervenes. We have found that the very best way to put adventure into marriage is to be involved together as a couple with God in his work. It certainly will not be boring. When I finished graduate school at the University of Texas, Gloria, our girls and I moved to Boston both to take my first job and to be a part of a church planting that hopefully would have impact in taking the gospel to New England. I loved my career in scientific research, and we loved our church group. I was a part of the Sperry Research Center, which was a small think tank that was located on a beautiful old four hundred acre estate just outside of Boston. The work was interesting, and the perks were great. The center was jokingly called "Sperry Country Club" because it was on a beautiful lake where we would swim, play tennis and jog on our lunch hour. I had a month of vacation each year, a great salary and benefits and a great retirement plan.While we loved our church group, it had very slow growth. We had some good friends in another church in Boston that was beginning to experience astounding numerical and spiritual growth. One day those friends invited us to breakfast and made a proposal that literally changed our lives forever. They challenged me to give up my career in physics and for both Gloria and me to go into the ministry fulltime with them! We prayed about it and got lots of advice for three months then I quit my job and entered the full-time ministry. I left my dream job with tremendous benefits to start a ministry with no track record, few benefits and no retirement program (I asked about retirement and was told, "We have a great retirement program; when you die, you go to heaven!") In May, when I made the announcement of my plans to leave Sperry the following September, some of my fellow employees thought I had lost my mind. One even said that I was going from physics to metaphysics. However, two months later, in July, the head of the research center called everyone together to announce that the research center was being closed. I was the only person in the whole center who had a job! We felt that this was God's exclamation point on our decision. That was thirty-five years ago; and that began one the most exciting adventures of our lives that took us all over the world helping in God's mission to seek and save the lost and created a lifetime of special memories.

The best part of memories is making them; the second-best part is remembering them. Today's adventures are the ones that will become tomorrow's special memories. As George Carlin said, "Life is not measured by the number of breaths we take, but by the moments that take our breath away." We urge you to put some creative thought, prayer and effort into making lots of great memories. It will pay double dividends: making them now and enjoying them later. Believe us, we are living midst the joy of fifty-six years of special memories!

Chapter Twenty-Two

KEEP ON DREAMING

"Now to him who is able to do immeasurably more than all we ask or imagine, according to his power that is at work within us, to him be glory in the church and in Christ Jesus throughout all generations, for ever and ever! Amen."
—Ephesians 3:20-21

Most of our adventures and memories began as dreams. Taking time to dream together is vitally important to keeping marriage alive and exciting.

Do you remember some of the dreams you had as a kid? They were wild, crazy and fun. Some of us were superman (and mom tied a bathroom towel around our neck so we could fly), and we went around taking down the bad guys. Or we were a princess with the prince finally carrying us away on his white horse, so we lived happily ever after. Or we were a doctor, a nurse, a fireman, a singer, an actor, or anything else that we might imagine. It was an amazing feeling, a fun time in life. In order to be it, all we had to do was dream it.

For most of us, as we grow up and "mature", we stop dreaming very much. The bills pile up, the hours are long and we are tired, the career isn't as exciting as we hoped, our princess or prince charming has a few warts, and we settle for a "normal" life. Why did it have to end? Does it have to end? We don't have to let life be something that just happens to us... we can live it! And to live it, we must dream it. There's nothing quite like being a dreamer and having wild visions of a life that you know you're going to live, even if you're not living it right now.

God is the original and ultimate dreamer. Think of everything that exists; the stars, the moon, the sun, animals, oceans, beaches, flowers, fruits. You and me... God's dream (Genesis 1-2). He was there before it all, just dreaming it up. How long did he think of the way the sun would feel on our skin, or the sound of the ocean, or the smell of rain? Imagine him thinking about how excited Adam was going to be the first time that he saw Eve; God had to smile just picturing it in his mind! And God dreamed up marriage, and the thrill it would bring to every couple who would enjoy it the way he designed for it to be enjoyed. But God's biggest dream is that we, the greatest of his creation who are created in his image, would love him with all our being.

A dream is just an inspiring picture of the future that energizes our heart and mind and motivates us to make it happen. It becomes a road map for us to follow. Dreams are valuable. They drive us forward. They give us energy. They make us enthusiastic. Dreaming is the opposite of simply drifting along, and it can be the difference between excitement and boredom.

Dreams motivate us and keep us from giving up in the hard times. A famous and obvious example is Martin Luther King with his famous "I have a dream!" speech. It was that dream that changed the way an entire nation thought and moved to action. If he did not first have a dream, he never would have stood up for what he believed. That is the power of dreams—to have hope and to try to change our present situation for the better.

Dreaming as an individual is important but dreaming as a married couple can be even more powerful. Jesus said, "Again, truly I tell you that if two of you on earth agree about anything they ask for, it will be done for them by my Father in heaven." (Matthew 18:19). Dreaming together as a couple can be one of the most exciting and uplifting things we do. After all, wasn't that a big part of what we did when we fell in love?

On Al and my very first date, we shared some of our dreams. That sparked an interest that only grew stronger from there, because we each had the identical dream of serving God and the church on the mission field. When we started steady dating, I used to write what my initials would be after we were married, GB, everywhere in Al's notebooks, and after we were engaged I would practice signing my new married name, Gloria Baird over and over!

We all begin our marriage with dreams. Oh yes, we remember them well! The hours we spend planning our wedding with excitement and imagining our honeymoon and then our future together. Nothing, not even being poor university students, dampen our enthusiasm for the plans and dreams we have for our years ahead. These discussions motivate us, connect us, and draw us together as we focus on trying to make our dreams become reality. That is the way life is for most of us; full of great dreams.

But what now? The wedding is a memory, the mortgage is a reality, the pressure of life is daily, and the kids are crying. But do we still dream together? Do we still imagine our future together? Or do we get stuck in the present? Does our vision get so limited by today's demands, chores and challenges that we aren't sure what direction we are going in anymore?

We are Country and Western music fans, and Tim McGraw is one of our favorite singers. One of his songs that speaks to the need for dreaming is *Live Like You Were Dying*.[1] The song describes a man in his forties who is diagnosed with a terminal disease and his response to facing death. His friend asks him how he is choosing to face the end.

> "He said,
> 'I was finally the husband
> That most of the time I wasn't
> And I became a friend a friend would like to have
> And all of a sudden going fishin'
> Wasn't such an imposition
> And I went three times that year I lost my dad
> I finally read the Good Book, and I
> Took a good, long, hard look
> At what I'd do if I could do it all again
> And then
> I went skydiving
> I went Rocky Mountain climbing
> I went 2.7 seconds on a bull named Fumanchu
> And I loved deeper
> And I spoke sweeter
> And I gave forgiveness I'd been denying'
> "And he said,
> 'Someday I hope you get the chance
> To live like you were dying."

Fortunately, we don't have to wait for a life-altering crisis to wake us up. But we do need to understand that dreaming about having an amazing life together is vitally important. It helps keep us on the same page so that we have something to look forward to as we work together as a team to make those dreams a reality. Dreaming together makes us excited about the future. And reaching our goals gives us another reason to celebrate in our marriage!

Here are some benefits of dreaming together:

- When you dream together, you grow together, not apart, because you are both moving toward the same future. And the journey and anticipation are often as exciting as the destination.

- It helps you focus on the positives instead of the negatives in life. Life has plenty of hard challenges. Even in bad times, your dreams can be the difference between sinking and swimming. Dreams help you to keep afloat since they show you a picture of how you would like the future to be.

- It gives you purpose. Life is constantly changing but having dreams that you are so connected with gives you the power to chase them and to never give up. It helps you define what is important in your life.

- It motivates you and drives you towards a goal. Having a dream that keeps you forward-looking can make you excited to get up in the morning.

- The unknown of following your dreams may spark a little healthy fear. Dreams can get the adrenalin flowing; they are the perfect cure for boredom. Following your dreams can make you feel more alive.

- The more you chase and accomplish your dreams that are based on God's priorities, the more you see God working in your life and realize that with Him nothing is impossible.

- Let us encourage you to sit down together and build some dreams together. They can be short term or long term. Ideally, get away together. Let your imagination run wild; the dreams don't need to be practical. Here are a few questions to get you thinking and talking together:

- When are you happiest?
- If we could spend a week together anywhere in the world, where would we go?
- What is your dream job?
- What has been the most exhilarating experience in your life?
- What is something wild you have always wanted to experience (sky diving, climb a mountain, hot air balloon ride, etc.)?
- What is your wildest dream?
- What is your biggest desire for our life as a whole?
- What do you hope for in our next year of marriage?
- What is the most meaningful thing we have accomplished together so far?
- What else would you like to accomplish together?
- If you could snap your fingers and have any one dream instantly become reality, what would it be?

Life is too short to settle for mediocre. Always be chasing a dream together.

END NOTES _____

1. Live Like You Were Dying, written by Tim Nicols and Craig Wiseman and sung by Tim McGraw. It reached No. 1 on the Billboard Country Charts and was voted Song of the Year in 2004.

Chapter Twenty-Three

FIND A GOOD MENTORING COUPLE

"Plans fail for lack of counsel,
but with many advisers they succeed."
—Proverbs 15:22

So far, we have discussed many things that are necessary for building a great marriage. Now, we add an essential ingredient; another couple.

When we married in 1961, we had never heard of pre-marriage counseling, marriage mentoring, discipling, or any other marriage aids that are common today. We were pretty much on our own. We could talk with our parents or our close married friends and we would occasionally get advice from them. But it is awkward to talk about sensitive subjects, like sex or finances, with your mom and dad or close friends. So, we learned a lot from our mistakes.

The Bible is filled with examples of mentoring: Eli and Samuel, Elijah and Elisha, Moses and Joshua, Naomi and Ruth, Barnabas and Paul, Paul and Timothy, etc. In so many areas of life, when a person wants to excel, they look for someone to help them. An Olympic athlete will move across the country to get the right coach. Students needing help in a subject will spend their scarce funds for a tutor. A person trying to get ahead in the business world will look for a mentor. Someone needing to get back in shape, lose those extra pounds and reduce their middle-aged spread will pay for a trainer at the gym. Doesn't it make sense that we seek help to ensure that the most important human relationship that we will ever have is going as well as it can? We believe that every married couple, regardless of age and experience, needs another couple in their life.

One of our most costly financial and spiritual mistakes

was buying a piece of land in ski country in New Hampshire. When we moved to New England after graduate school, we were determined to enjoy the long winters, so we as a family started snow skiing. What better way to enjoy the winter that to own a chalet in ski country? We decided that we could buy the land and build the chalet ourselves on the weekends. The land was a two-hour drive from home, so we decided that we would make it a family affair every weekend. We would take a different family from church with us each week, and they could help us build it. That way we could all have our Sunday worship together on our land, and we wouldn't be missing church.

It was a very unwise idea from several standpoints. To have spent all of our spare time during the week planning and buying materials, to have taken every spare weekend for months for our entire family, to have attempted to build a house with no previous experience and to have taken that amount of time away from the church family would have taken a huge toll on our family. We got no advice before buying the land or coming up with the idea of construction. Fortunately, we came to our senses before we started building recognizing that we would have exhausted ourselves physically, financially, and spiritually. We eventually sold the land at a loss but learned a valuable lesson about the need for advice.

For years we have done a lot of marriage counseling among Christians. After a while, we began to see the same pattern over and over, so now we start off the very first session with a couple by asking them these two questions: 1) "How is your relationship with God?" and 2) "Who is in your life helping the two of you?" These questions are rhetorical, because we already know what their answers will be before they even respond: "My relationship with God is not very good lately" and "No one is in our life helping us with our marriage." We hear very few exceptions to those answers. That is where we begin. If they have a poor relationship with God, we cannot help them until it changes because that is where they must start. And then they need to get a married couple to help them for the long haul.

Long ago, we noticed that life-long patterns and habits are formed in marrieds in their first year of marriage. So, we began a mentoring group for each of the couples in our church immediately after their honeymoon, which we continued for many years. We met once a month as a group, and each couple "graduated" from the group after they had been in it for a year. That was one of the most enjoyable things that we did in any given month.

The couples came in eager to learn and very quickly became friends with all of the members. When we first started, we were surprised at how open and vulnerable each person quickly became within the group. While we usually had a lesson about some aspect of marriage that would be helpful to them, we soon learned that they were eager to share and ask questions.

Usually at least one of the couples has just had a "bump" that they some need advice about. Initially we would field those questions, but then we decided to let the rest of the group give their advice first. We were amazed at the wise advice that the other newly-married couples could give. It was an important lesson for all of us in the group: even a newlywed can give good advice when they are not emotionally involved. It just added evidence to our conviction that every married couple needs to have another couple regularly involved in their marriage.

There are many advantages to having a couple in our life. Here are a few:

1. Having another couple praying for our marriage daily. Nothing helps as much as having God to guide our relationship.

2. No couple is totally objective about themselves; we certainly aren't, especially during our times of disagreement and hurt. In those non-objective times, we need people who can help us see more clearly.

3. The wife is to be in submission to the leadership of her husband. It is very securing to the wife to know that someone is in her husband's life, calling him to be sensitive and righteous; and that she can call for help when she is stuck, or he is just being a jerk.

4. We have access to wisdom that we may not have yet. Having someone who has been married longer than us or people who are at least a few steps ahead of us in a specific struggle can help so much. It just makes sense to learn from the mistakes of others, rather than

to make our own. We will take plenty of wrong turns in life; but each one we avoid makes the journey more enjoyable.

5. While our mother and father can certainly help us, they usually do not have the objectivity that a mentor couple has.

6. We have someone who can help us see how our actions impacts our spouse. Sometimes we think we have the greatest idea and the perfect solution. Having a mentor to bounce these ideas off can provide insight into ways our mate may be affected by our idea or action. When someone else looks at our scenario from a different angle, we get a feel of what it might be like to be on the other side.

7. We have someone who can help us set and examine our priorities. Having a marriage mentor enables another couple to see where there may be problem areas in how we're setting our priorities and spending our time. Having someone ask us consistently how we are investing in our relationship with each other and with God keeps us accountable for making the right choices. This would have helped us so much in our plans and investment in the ski property in New Hampshire that we previously described.

8. We have a cheering section who is encouraging us every day (Hebrews 3:13). The couple can point out where we've been and where we are right now, highlighting the positive changes we've made, the areas of growth where we have excelled, and old behaviors each of us have left behind. These encouraging words of victory are very helpful to keeping us going.

9. We have a sounding board. Our couple can be safe places for us to express ourselves and have them play back to us what they are hearing us say. It is surprising how often just saying something out loud brings clarity to our thoughts and helps us see if they have validity.

Hopefully, this list of advantages convinces you to find a mentor couple, if you don't already have one. The next step is to find that couple. Here are some things to look for in the couple:

1. They need to have an outstanding walk with God. Their role is not to fix you, but to point you to God and help you rely on him. Without God, nothing will end up well.

2. They need to have a good (not perfect) marriage that you admire. There is no point in choosing a couple who doesn't have strengths in their relationship that you want to imitate and will model for you. They can't lead you to a place they haven't first gone to.

3. They need to be at least a little ahead of you in life. They don't have to have all the answers but can help you find the answers.

4. Ideally, they will be in the same church group as you, so that you will at least see each other every week. The relationship will go even deeper if you talk or text several times a week.

5. You need to be totally honest with them and to grow in the relationship with them to the point that you can share or talk about any aspect of your marriage with them. including sexual issues. And they need to be comfortable with that.

6. They need to be willing to be open, transparent and vulnerable with you about their mistakes, struggles and sins. That is where the real growth comes from in the mentoring relationship and to be able to learn from their growing areas.

7. They must be good listeners.

8. And finally, they must expect you to grow and change, and pray for you daily to have victories. They need to be able to gently challenge you to change and hold you accountable for those changes.

No one area that we discuss in this book is going to ensure a successful, happy marriage; and other than the relationship with God, it is hard to prioritize them. But, the need for a mentoring relationship must come near the top of the list.

Chapter Twenty-Four

HANDLE YOUR
FINANCES RESPONSIBLY

"But godliness with contentment is great gain. For we brought nothing into the world, and we can take nothing out of it. But if we have food and clothing, we will be content with that. People who want to get rich fall into temptation and a trap and into many foolish and harmful desires that plunge men into ruin and destruction."
—1 Timothy 6:6-9

Money issues are the number one cause of stress in marriage, according to a survey by SunTrust Bank.[1] In 2014, in another study, *Money Magazine*[2] polled over one thousand married adults ages twenty-five and over with household incomes above $50,000 to find out how couples manage their finances once they tied the knot. Survey results showed that seventy percent of couples argued about money more than household chores, togetherness, sex, personal tastes and everything else. Having financial arguments is a major predictor of divorce, a separate study by Kansas State University found. On the plus side, the *MONEY Magazine* survey revealed that couples who trust their partner with finances felt more secure, argued less, and had more fulfilling sex lives.

Many arguments that we have may seem like they are about the money issues we are dealing with at the time. But, they may be about a clash of temperaments and our differing views of spending money, shaped by our upbringing and other life circumstances instead. This can be referred to as our "money personality," the way we naturally tend to handle money. It is not a skill, such as making a budget or balancing a checkbook, but rather the way we think about finances. For example, you might be a spender, a saver, a risk taker or a security seeker. No one personality is more desirable than another; each has its own strengths and weaknesses.

It is very helpful to understand the views our parents had about money. Were they frugal or big spenders? Did they live on a budget? Did they talk about money? What is your mate's greatest fear with your finances? These things shape how we view money today. A very useful couple's activity is to sit down and have a mutual sharing time to explore and understand each other's money personality, including questions like "What's your first money memory?" or "How did you spend your allowance?" or "What's the best thing you learned about money from your parents?"

As with every aspect of our marriage, the starting place in building the financial part of our lives together is God. And his approach to our finances is very different from that of the world. Francis Bacon, an English philosopher, statesman, scientist, jurist, orator, and author in the late 1500s wrote, "Money is like manure. It's not good unless it is spread around." God wants to use our financial resources to advance his kingdom and help others, as well as to provide for our needs. As we blend together the financial pieces of our two lives as singles into one unified piece, God makes it very simple: it is not putting "my" finances together with "your" finances, but rather merging God's finances that he has entrusted to each of us. Together we become stewards and managers of what always been God's. Interestingly, Jesus spoke more about money than he did about any other topic, and even more than his teachings on heaven and hell combined. Why did money matter so much to him? Because it reflects our attitude towards God.

For a couple to be unified, we must have the same priorities. And our top priority must be loving God. Once we agree on that, setting other priorities becomes much simpler. In Matthew 6:33, Jesus promised: "Seek first the kingdom of God and his righteousness, and all these things will be added to you." That one promise can remove so much stress from our marriage, knowing that God will take care of his end of the agreement if we maintain the right priorities.

After setting the priorities, we need to develop a plan to turn the priorities into reality. Unfortunately, most couples are naïve when it comes to financial planning. Surveys show that fewer than one out of five couples even know how to balance their bank accounts. They don't know how much money they have to spend or where it goes.

Here are some practical ideas that we have found useful in managing finances responsibly:

1. *Give to God first and live on the rest.*
Even as poor university students, we tithed. At the very start of our marriage we set a goal of giving more back to God each month than we spent on any other budget area, such as rent or car payment. Eating beans and cornbread wasn't so bad. We learned in those early-marriage years that we couldn't out-give God, and that lesson has stuck with us ever since.

2. *Set up a working household budget.*
It's the most effective way to keep track of your money; however, only one in three couples have one, according to a Gallup poll. And having a budget is useless unless you record and categorize your income and expenses. We find that many marrieds that we counsel fund their monthly expenses from ATM machines without recording where the money was spent, and as a result have no idea where it all went at the end of the month.
We advise getting a good budgeting software program and entering all expenses every day; it is just too hard to remember them after a few days. We began doing this when we were first married in 1961; and back then there were no personal computers, so we wrote down everything in a budget book. We still have those books; it is fun to look back at them and remember when we had so little and had so much fun. We wouldn't have made it financially as poor university students if we hadn't worked our budget. But just knowing where the money goes is only half of the battle.

3. *Tweak the budget every month.*
The real victories start coming when at the end of each month you sit down together and see how your actual expenses compared with the budget for the month. From that, you can modify the budget for the next month.

4. *Do not have separate bank accounts.*

When you marry, you become one; merge your finances unless you have a very unusual set of circumstances. In that case, get advice from a godly, competent couple or professional.

5. *Set a limit of what either of you can spend without the agreement of both of you before you spend it.*

6. *Budget a "fun money" amount for both of you each month that is yours to spend any way you want without the other's approval.*

7. *Use a credit card only for convenience, and totally pay off the debt each month.*

Do not accumulate credit card interest. If you don't have the self-control to do this, cut up your card. The high interest rate of the unpaid balance of credit cards can wreck your financial plan and waste the money that really belongs to God.

8. *Start saving for retirement as soon as possible.*

9. *The compounding effect of early saving is huge fifty years later. We didn't, but now we wish that someone had advised us to do that.*

Learn to live on less than you earn. It is a dangerous trap to believe that we deserve to have all the things in early marriage that our parents worked for years to have. Some of our best memories were our early years together when we had very little, and most of what we had, we bought used. Be thankful for what you have, not discontent about what you don't have.

10. *Get out of debt and stay out of debt.*

Save until you can afford a purchase, except for major items like a car or house.

11. *In your budget, allow for expenses that may not occur monthly, such as auto insurance, home owner or rental insurance, special contribution, vacation, etc.*

12. *Have an emergency fund. Things will happen that you don't plan on.*

13. *Get lots of advice.*

Talk to financially-responsible disciples. Use some excellent commercial resources such as *Financial Peace University* or *Crown Financial Ministries*.

14. *Use pay raises to give more sacrificially (a tithe should be a floor, not a ceiling of our giving), to pay off debt, etc.*

We decided at the beginning of our marriage that as God blessed us with more income, we were not entitled to raise our lifestyle at the same rate. Rather we committed to use the additional money to help the church and other individuals while raising our standard of living at a slower rate. We believe that in making and keeping that commitment, God has showered his blessings on us in countless incredible ways throughout our years together.

God and Satan continually war in our hearts and minds for control of our material wealth and the battle never ends. Surrender to God in this area of our marriage is essential for building the marriage that we all long for. Having a god-focused, working financial plan is key to godliness and contentment.

Chapter Twenty-Five

TRAIN YOUR CHILDREN

*"Children are a heritage from the LORD,
offspring a reward from him.
Like arrows in the hands of a warrior
are children born in one's youth.
Blessed is the man
whose quiver is full of them."*
—Psalm 127:3-5

We realize that not everyone reading this book will have children; but most will at some point in their marriage. Children are a gift from God, but a gift that has a profound shaping-effect on any marriage.

Through the years, many younger parents have asked us for advice about parenting. The top of our list is to tell them to have the goal of raising them to love God. Key in this is molding their hearts, not just their actions. Since this a book primarily about marriage, we can devote only this chapter to rearing children, when an entire book is really needed. So, we will skim the surface as we explain a few of our convictions.

GOD IS THE ONLY TRUSTWORTY AUTHORITY ON REARING CHILDREN

We have lived long enough to see the trends about child rearing change several times. We were raising our girls during the Dr. Spock era, only later finding out that some of his theories were not the best. Many of you have not even heard of Dr. Spock since many other 'experts' have long since replaced him. Fortunately, we knew there were principles that we could depend on to be effective and unchangeable from the one true expert—God.

We are concerned that we see many Christian parents rejecting clear-cut directions from the Bible, such as spanking. "Do not withhold discipline from a child; if you punish him with the rod, he will not die. Punish him with the rod and save his soul from death." (Proverbs 23:13-14). Certainly, spanking should never be done in anger and should be age appropriate, but do not let some modern parenting guru persuade you that Biblical parenting wisdom is passé. Many good books are available that explain the "how-tos and whys" of proper godly discipline. Anyone who believes that God's manual, the Bible, is outdated, will make some serious mistakes in rearing their children.

BE UNIFIED

You are better as a couple that either of you would be individually. If I had been parenting by myself, I would have been too firm, while Gloria would have been too soft and sentimental. Together we found a good balance. In areas of opinion it would be better to do something that may not be the absolute best choice than to choose the best option but not be united. The kids will try hard to divide you to get their own way; and they are masters at knowing which parent will most likely let them have their way at any point in time.

BE CONSISTENT

Don't change your rules and expectations without a good reason. Being tired or in a hurry is not a good reason. Children will be confused if parents are not consistent. Imagine how confused a driver would be if one day it was legal to run a red light, but the next day he got a ticket for running through the same red light. It is easier to be consistent if you make as few rules as possible but enforce those rules implicitly.

PRACTICE WHAT YOU PREACH

Make God the center of your home in a genuine way. Children are like little video cameras, recording everything. They learn by example, even more than what we say. Kids hate hypocrisy. Once I (Gloria) was preparing to teach a parenting class with our oldest daughter Staci. I asked her what had helped her the most growing up in our home. She said, "What I saw you and Dad being at home was the same as I saw you being outside of the home."

TEACH AND MODEL THE SETTING OF PRIORITIES AND SACRIFICE

Jesus says that we cannot be his disciples if we don't put God and his kingdom first. Our kids know if we do or not, if they are old enough. Sometime ask your older kids what they see as your top priorities. Hopefully, they see that the top of our list includes our love for God and his church, our love for each other and our kids, and our determination for us to get to heaven and to take our kids with us, and to take as many others with us as we can. An important ingredient in that is our sacrifice of our time and money.

We will not inspire our kids by living in the comfort zone. Too many kids see their parents putting the job, the kids' sports or other interests above the church. Most churches have times of special financial contributions; these are excellent opportunities to teach sacrifice. We would talk to the kids about what expenses, such as eating out, that we could reduce as the time for the contribution grew closer. We had a large vegetable garden and our special contribution was in September, so we tried to have most of our meals from the garden for the entire month of August. That way we could give all the money we had saved from our food budget.

MODEL AND EXPECT RESPECT

What a person says and does is of prime importance in communicating respect, and the person's tone of voice and body language also play an essential part. My (Gloria) mother used to say, "You will always love your kids, but no one else will unless you teach them to be respectful!"

TEACH AND EXPECT OBEDIENCE

Obedience is a fundamental building block in anyone building a relationship with God and it is one that the kids must learn in order to have a functional, loving family. Failing to teach obedience to the kids when they are young will probably doom you to "reap the whirlwind" in their teen years. If you wonder what your child will be as a teenager, look at him at two then multiply that by eight, and you have a sixteen-year-old! Our kids use this guideline with their children: "First time, every time, and with a good attitude.' We learned the hard way that counting "1... 2...3", expecting them to obey by the time we reach "3" teaches the child that he doesn't have to obey until you get to "2 1/2."

VALUE THE FAMILY MEALS

Study after study,[1] even secular studies, show many tremendous benefits to the kids and the parents, too, of having regular family meals together. The entire family sits down at the dinner table for the entire length of the meal, with no TV, no cell phones, and no other distractions. They become one of, if not the most important communication time for the entire family. Everyone can share about the highlights of their day and anything else that comes up. We also would usually read a scripture and have a very short devotional.

We learn from 2 Timothy 3:15 that Timothy began learning the scriptures from infancy. So, we as a family learned one Bible verse each week, and any of us, including the kids, could ask anyone else to quote the verse, or any verse we had learned in the past. It was a lot of fun, and we all can still remember some of those verses decades later. In addition, once a week, we would have a family night, which not only included the meal, but games and other activities. Each of our three girls, when they were old enough, would take turns cooking and preparing the meal.

DON'T TRY TO LIVE THROUGH YOUR KIDS

It is all too common to see parents who try to get their kids to excel in mom or dad's favorite sports or other activities. Often this happens because the parent wished they had excelled themselves and now wants to live vicariously through their child. This is both selfish and harmful to the kids. You, the parent, had your chance; now let the kids have theirs.

PRACTICE HOSPITALITY

Hospitality is an important part of the Christian life, and there is no better way to teach it to the kids than for them to experience it firsthand. Our home was "Grand Central Station." Our girls usually had some friends over, and we had many guests. Some lived with us for short periods of time. It was not unusual for us to have a couple who we were trying to help with some serious marriage problem, or even occasionally someone coming down from a drug high. Looking back, this had an unexpected positive benefit to our kids as they were able to see firsthand in a safe environment how bad life can be when someone doesn't follow God's way.

MOM & DAD'S RELATIONSHIP IS STILL THE MOST IMPORTANT

Next to God, our relationship is the most important. Yes, even more important than the kids. We often tell parents, "You love your children better when you love your mate best." It is significant that various studies show that building a better marriage results in being better parents.[2] Make sure you are getting special alone time together, at home and away. Put a lock on your bedroom door. Generally, the kids don't belong in your bed. Evangelist and author Sam Laing says, "The marriage bed is intended for two things and the kids don't help either."

It is comforting to know that we do not have to be perfect parents. We will make mistakes. We and our children will learn and grow through them—they won't be ruined by them. God is the ultimate Father who is molding and shaping all of us. He will work even through mistakes if we are humble toward him and others, and if we keep loving our children. Love does cover a multitude of sins. Enjoy every stage. Children grow up so fast! Be sure to treasure the times you have with them. Make memories that will be treasured for years to come.

Oh, yes. It is never over. Just when you think you have finished raising the kids, the best is yet to come—GRANDKIDS!

END NOTES _____

1. "The Value of Family Meals," September 14, 2017, https://firstthings.org/the-value-of-family-meals.

2. Sue Johnson, *Hold Me Tight* (Little, Brown and Company, 2008), 261.

Chapter Twenty-Six

APPRECIATE THE STAGES OF MARRIAGE

"Place me like a seal over your heart,
like a seal on your arm;
for love is as strong as death,
its jealousy unyielding as the grave.
It burns like blazing fire,
like a mighty flame.
Many waters cannot quench love;
rivers cannot sweep it away.
If one were to give
all the wealth of one's house for love,
it would be utterly scorned."
—Song of Songs 8:6-7

Just as we discussed in the previous chapter on children, things keep on changing in marriage. We go through stages with each different from the last. The challenge is to enjoy each stage and to constantly grow.

The psychologist Paul Tournier said, "I've been married six times—all to the same woman." Tournier explained that he never got divorced, but rather his marriage transitioned from one stage to another. As strange as that may sound, we all go through different stages in our marriage, just like everyone, married or not, goes through stages in life. The way we adapt individually and to each other in each stage will have a profound effect on the quality of our marriage. Every couple on their wedding day hopes that their love for each other will make their marriage last forever. But when wives were asked a few years after the wedding if they would marry the same man again, almost six out of ten say no, according to a book by Susan Shapiro Barash, *The Nine Stages Of Marriage*,[1] in which she interviewed more than two hundred women aged between twenty-one and eight-five.

In this chapter we will describe four of the most common stages in marriage that we have experienced ourselves and observed in other couples, some of the characteristics of each stage, and what we have learned about how to enjoy them.

By discussing these stages, we want to help minimize the adjustment issues by preparing you to lay the proper groundwork for mutual understanding and realistic expectations. With these stages in mind, you can see how important it is to begin the process of preparation as early as possible in your marriage.

The starting point in navigating each stage is to remember two basic absolutes: God comes first in everything, and the two of you together are to be the top priority in human relationships. If you hang on to these two keys, you are well on your way to being successful in each stage. God intends to give us unique blessings in each stage, and Satan has his plans to sabotage all that God wants to accomplish. If we are patient and follow God's path, each stage will in several ways make our marriage more rewarding and stronger.

BEGINNINGS

This is the honeymoon stage. This is the stage that Solomon describes in Song of Songs 2:4, *"Let him lead me to the banquet hall, and let his banner over me be love."* Couples begin to develop a strong sense of "we" and are head-over-heals in love. The first few years are exhilarating as they experience many new "firsts" together; their first apartment, their first Christmas as a married couple, their first joint bank account and tax return, to name a few. At the same time, the early years require some radical personal adjustment, which can stressful on the relationship. According to research done by the Center for Marriage and Family at Creighton University (2000), the top three issues for couples during these first few years of marriage are time, sex, and money.

Most newlyweds struggle to balance schedules between themselves individually and as a couple, daily time with God and church, with friends and extended family, and work. Sex should be the gloriously easy and fun part, but most couples should make sure to work out the frequency and techniques of pleasing each other. Many newlyweds are at the beginning of their earnings curve in their careers. They are also learning to understand and blend their individual attitudes toward money. In addition, many couples bring school loans and other significant debt into the marriage.

The first year of marriage is pivotal in building the proper foundation for what will shape the following years; habits are formed then that will mold the future relationship. We strongly urge (yes, even insist) young couples whom we influence to begin praying together every day, for the rest of their lives. They also need all the help and advice they can get and that is why we encourage couples to set up a mentoring relationship with another couple whose marriage and spirituality they admire, and who are ahead of them in life experience. (See Chapter 23 on mentoring.)

AND BABY MAKE THREE

Introducing children into the marriage mix is tremendously exciting. The thrill of "making" a baby together is one of God's unique gifts to a couple. (Of course, not every baby is planned. Our first baby wasn't but making him was still a lot of fun!) The point is that having a child as a result of our love for each other, and having the baby be a unique combination of the two of us is to experience one of God's truly amazing blessings. Also, many couples choose to adopt, which is no less one of God's great blessings.

The move to parenthood from the honeymoon stage is a giant leap forward. Children bring joy and responsibility. Without the proper spiritual and emotional preparation, life can quickly become overwhelming. One of the biggest adjustments is that your marriage no longer revolves around just the two of you. Parents can feel overwhelmed with the responsibility of caring for a child, as well as with their loss of privacy and freedom. In addition to the time-consuming demands of changing diapers and feeding at all hours, questions of who should assume which responsibilities, parenting styles, not to mention the issue of making room in the relationship for this seemingly all-consuming new priority, can all become exhausting.

You must avoid the all-to common temptation for the father to retreat into his career and fall into the role of "workaholic" while the mother assumes the "nurturing" role. Parenting needs both parents; work hard to build a team. Hopefully, your shared pleasure in having a child offsets the loss of time just for the two of you that you had before, and that you've made a commitment to carve out some special couple time on a regular basis so that you can remain lovers as well as partners in parenting. Couples who don't intentionally strategize and plan to keep their intimacy strong can begin to feel alienated and drift apart. This stage should and can be very rewarding as you move from the couple-only to family time of life, but it takes a lot of work.

SCHOOL DAYS

We remember how nervous all of us were the first day of school for each of our kids—the kids and well as us parents! We had been getting them ready for it for five years; how would they do without us? And they did just fine. That is what parenting is all about: preparing our kids to thrive in the real world outside of the safety of our home. And, hopefully helping them grow a faith in God that will guide them throughout their life adventure. It is so important during these years at school to build effective, open communication for the entire family. We are strong believers in family meals and a family night with the whole family together and this includes no TV, no cell phones, no computers. That did as much to build closeness in our family as anything we did. Also, we found that all three of our girls would talk very vulnerably at bedtime. School activities, homework and extracurricular activities can create a very complicated and hectic schedule. It is important to not let life and the schedule control you; continually evaluate your priorities.

THE EMPTY NEST

We will not say very much about the empty nest in this chapter because we have an entire chapter devoted to it. (See Chapter 26 on the empty nest.) What we will say is that this for us has been probably the most fun stage of our marriage; it is our second honeymoon, except this time we know much more how to enjoy it. Sometimes, though, a couple who happily thought they were in the empty-nest stage are faced with a boomerang young adult who again needs their care, presence, home, and perhaps babysitting services. An added plus is that this is the stage of having grandkids. Until you experience the joy of having grandkids curl up on your lap, or tell you they love you, or want to play "hide and go seek," you cannot begin to imagine the joy these little rascals bring. For most couples, this is the longest stage in terms of years, and may well be longer than all of the other stages combined. These later years will also include some periods of sadness: the loss of parents and possibly some personal major health issues. For us, during this stage we lost both sets of parents, and Gloria has had to deal with stage four cancer. Even with that, we would still pick this stage as our favorite.

Circumstances will vary for each couple as you take this journey through life together. The two of us look at it as our adventure which has lasted for more than five and a half decades. There are exciting parts, fun parts, funny parts, hard parts, sad parts and scary parts. The challenge has been and is to enjoy every stage. God has gone with us each step of the way, and each step has made us more in love with him and with each other. We can't ask for more than that!

Chapter Twenty-Seven

ENJOY THE EMPTY NEST

*"There is a time for everything,
and a season for every activity
under the heavens."*
—Ecclesiastes 3:1

We had been looking forward to this day for a long time. Staci, our oldest was about to begin her freshman year of college 1500 miles away from home and this was an exciting time for the whole family. A significant cause of rejoicing was that Kristi and Keri could now each have their own bedroom. We all enjoyed the road trip in our station wagon packed to the gills with all of Staci's stuff. After three days of driving, Staci was settled in her dorm room and had made some new friends. The four of us said our good-byes to Staci and piled into the car for the long drive home.

We did okay for the first five miles; then all four of us started bawling! Life as we knew it would not be the same with only the four of us left at home. For the next six years the nest continued to empty. Each time one left for college, we felt a hole in our family, especially when we looked at their empty chair at the dinner table. We also missed having their friends around, which was almost always. And then came the day that just the two of us were left and now we were "empty-nesters."

THE JOYS OF THE EMPTY NEST

We like to refer to this time in life as the second honeymoon, or even as the real honeymoon. Someone has humorously said that the honeymoon is wasted on newlyweds! And to some extent, that is true, because we know so much more about each other and how to please each other than we did at the beginning. It didn't take long for us to adjust to the empty house. No longer did we need to close the bedroom door, be concerned about being heard at inopportune times or choose our time for intimacy (or even the room). Without a doubt these are the best years of our physical relationship.

Hopefully, by this point in life your mate is already your best friend. (See Chapter 6 on friendship.) For some of you, this is not true. Some even think, "I don't even feel like I know my mate. We haven't been alone since I was in our twenties; the kids have always been with us. Our whole life revolved around the kids. Now what will we talk about at the dinner table?" If this describes you, it is time to start building the kind of marriage that God intends for you to have. Taking time each day to talk about each other's ups and downs of the day is a good beginning. Some couples take a daily walk together. Others sit on the patio after work.

Communicate on a vulnerable level, sharing your important thoughts and feelings regularly; that helps to reconnect, and bonding occurs. Allowing yourself to grieve the loss of the roles of parenting years is a healthy start to new growth. Discussing openly the strengths and limitations of your relationship and setting new goals together will help. Forgiving old hurts and resentments is a necessary step towards building the marriage that God wants us to have. Getting other couples to help with these struggles is often just what is needed.

Parenting does not stop when the kids leave home. Just because they leave doesn't mean they don't need us anymore... it's quite the opposite. The relationship just looks different than it did while they were still at home. The direct instruction and oversight morphs into advice giving (and sometimes being given advice from our now-mature kids) and friendship. Regardless of whether our kids are in college or working in a distant country, with modern technology we are just a cell call, text, or FaceTime away. And sometimes they may even be in the next room, because it isn't unusual for our kids to move back home and sometimes with their own kids!

They may need us more than ever, just in different ways. We knew our girls were going to need our help and encouragement (and money) after they left home, but we thought that our job as parents was done when the last of out three girls was married. "Now she is her husband's responsibility", we thought. WRONG!

Our responsibilities had just doubled. Now instead of three girls, we had three couples. And then their kids came, so now it isn't just six, but those six plus nine grandkids. And are grandkids ever worth the wait! Someone has rightly said, "If we had known grandkids were so much fun, we would have bypassed our kids and just started with them!"

THE CHALLENGES

God does not intend for any of the marriage stages to be downers, but for each stage to be filled with rich blessings. For sure there will be challenges, but challenges are meant to help us grow. Certainly, the empty-nest stage is one of the more challenging. Many years later after all three of our girls had married and we had moved to the west coast from Boston, we all went back together with the new sons-in-law to see our little three bedroom house where our girls grew up (with just one bathroom, if you can imagine four women and one bathroom). We had thought we might see if the present owners would let us look around inside, but when we drove up and saw the house none of us wanted to go in. It was a very strange feeling. It was the same house, but the house didn't hold the memories; our hearts did (and still do). In that house we shared laughter, tears, victories, defeats, joy and adventures. Sometimes, we wish we could roll the clock back to those very special years in that house. That is some of the emotion of the empty nest.

When you've spent decades actively parenting, it takes some adjusting to settle into the new lifestyle of the empty nest. The pain of having all the kids leaving home can be so severe to some that a legitimate condition develops called the "empty nest syndrome". While this is not a clinical condition, the feelings of loneliness, grief and uselessness are not unusual and can result in worry, stress, loss of purpose, and even depression. The syndrome is especially common in stay-at-home mothers who have spent so much of their energies on the kids for years, but now wonder what their purpose is. But every parent feels the transition to some extent.

THE OPPORTUNITIES

We believe that this stage can and should be the one in which our lives have the greatest impact. Statistics tell us that, chances are, more than half of our married life remains once all the kids leave home; so that makes the empty nest the longest of the stages of marriage in terms of years. You probably have several decades of life ahead of you, and it's important to ask God to give you some direction on how he wants to use you during those years. This is a good time to ask, "What is our mission for this final stage of our life?" Many things set you up to have lives that really count. A few are:

1. You have lived enough years to have developed a mature walk with God. You have seen Him deliver you through the hard challenges enough times to have developed a trust in Him.

2. You have a life partner that you have bonded with which enables you to be a strong team.

3. You have parented children which has taught you many things about life and relationships.

4. Now that you have an empty nest, you have much more time than when you were raising the kids. Hopefully you will use it for more than hobbies, travel or watching your favorite TV shows.

5. You have probably advanced in your careers to the point that you have enough money to help others and to fund your works for God.

6. You have lived long enough to have grown in your wisdom by making countless stupid mistakes and learning from God through the trials and troubles of life.

All these things, and more, mean that the best is yet to come if we surrender our lives to him and follow his direction.

Beyond empty nesting is retirement. At this point, without kids at home and full-time employment, there are countless possibilities for serving God and his churches around the world. We have several friends who have gone for a year to help in smaller churches; one couple even spent a year helping in South Africa. Another couple is supporting themselves financially as they lead a small church here in Arizona. Why not plan on using your hard-earned wisdom and finances to have the adventure of a lifetime by helping in places that could use your talents and experience?

There is no limit to the new opportunities that are available to empty-nest couples; and in planning for and pursuing these ventures together, your marriage will thrive. Ask God to give you wisdom and watch Him work in ways that will go beyond your plans and even beyond your dreams.

Chapter Twenty-Eight

SHARE WHAT YOU HAVE

"Therefore go and make disciples
of all nations, baptizing them in the
name of the Father and of the Son
and of the Holy Spirit..."
—Matthew 28:19-20

A book on marriage would not be complete without a discussion of God's mission for us as individuals and as couples to make disciples. With us building great marriages, we can be a light to those around us, pointing them to God.

God has designed the plan to bring a messed-up world back to him and desperately wants everyone to have the opportunity to respond. We believe that God intends for our marriages and families to be a key part of reconciling the world back to himself. There are three parts to the plan that we want to discuss in this chapter: (1) raise our kids so they want to become Christians; (2) convert non-Christian spouses; and (3) use the family to help others find God.

LEADING OUR KIDS TO CHRIST

Next to us as husband and wife going to heaven, our priority is to do everything we can to take our kids with us. We believe that the first and most important step is to surrender the kids to God. We once heard an Irish preacher, Jim McGuiggan, tell about his and his wife's parenting of their kids. He said that they as parents, like most parents, would pray for the safety of their kids. Then one day he realized that he didn't need to tell God what his kids needed; God knew far better than they did. From that time forward they began to pray that God would take whatever action was needed for their kids to live lives devoted to him, even sickness, drug addiction or prostitution! McGuiggan's convictions changed us and from then on we have tried to surrender our kids to God's will. Certainly, that does not mean that we have not tried to be wise in drawing boundaries for them.

God created the family as the perfect incubator for our kid's faith. Normally we have them for at least seventeen years which are their most formative years. They are learning machines and video cameras. They see our actions; they know our values; they know our strengths and weaknesses, they know our priorities. Hopefully, we make time to teach them, pray with them, and listen to them. Family meals, family devotionals, prayer times and fun times are all vital. And it is important to help them develop friendships with the kids at church who are good influences. But, as important as those things are, they will fall short if we as parents are not living as the example that we want our kids to imitate. Al and I were so thankful and humbled when our oldest daughter, Staci, who is a strong Christian mother and was teaching a parenting class with me, shared that a major thing that helped her decide to be a Christian was seeing her mom and dad be the same people at home that we were away from home. Our kids are watching us and will choose either to imitate our faith or reject it.

THE NON-CHRISTIAN MATE

One great challenge to having a great marriage is for the husband and wife to not be united on the most important thing in life, God. All the other major decisions and priorities follow from that top priority. I (Al) grew up in a home where my mom was a Christian and my dad was not. He was a great dad, and he had tremendous morals, but he and my mom were not united on how to serve God. When I was a teen, I saw her cry many tears about where my dad was spiritually; and she urged me over and over to only marry a Christian. (My dad did become a Christian later in life, but it was after my mom had died.)

I witnessed firsthand why God inspired Paul to write in 2 Corinthians 6:14, *"Do not be yoked together with unbelievers."* It is quite common for either the husband or wife to be converted after they were married and to eagerly desire and pray for them both to be united in Christ. We want to share two stories that we witnessed firsthand with happy endings, one for the husband becoming a Christian first and the other, the wife. The names and some details have been changed to protect the couples' privacy.

Bill and Jan were a talented young professional couple with a young child. Bill was doing his medical residency, and Jan was on a career fast track with a large company. Bill was invited to a Bible study group, and he eagerly went. He studied the Bible and was baptized. Jan was less than excited, especially when she understood Bill's radical change in priorities and his new time commitments in his already tight schedule as a resident. Before long, things got so tense that one-night Bill came home to find that Jan had dumped his clothes in the front yard! Things remained so difficult at home that Bill seriously considered giving up on God and the church. Fortunately, he had some strong disciples in his life who encouraged him to persevere. They also helped him to be a better husband and to be more considerate of Jan's feelings. Months later, after things had calmed down, a married couple in the church who Jan knew and liked asked her to study the Bible. Jan didn't make it easy; she said she would only do it if the couple would come and study at 6 am every week! They did, and finally Jan was baptized almost a year after Bill. That was years ago. Since that time, they have all three children who are strong Christians, they have converted their parents, and they have led countless others to Christ.

Ed and Flo were long-term natives of their town, as were their parents. Flo was invited to church, she came and began studying the Bible. Ed didn't approve, especially after she was baptized. He did everything he could to put obstacles in her way. He would hide the keys to her car when it was time to go to church. That didn't work, because her friends would pick her up. Finally, Ed issued an ultimatum: "It is either me or God, you have to choose!" Flo said, "Ed, I really do love you, but if you force me to choose, I will choose God." Ed said for the first time, he realized how serious Flo was about her Christianity. He decided that if it meant that much to her, he had better check it out. He did, he studied and was baptized. Their decision totally changed their life and their marriage for the better. Today, years later they are lights to their community because of their Christian service and their marriage.

In both cases, and in most situations, the thing that matters the most in the conversion of a mate is the loving behavior of the disciple and unbending commitment to God and his church. This is the point that Peter makes for wives in 1 Peter 3:1-2, "Wives, in the same way submit yourselves to your own husbands so that, if any of them do not believe the word, they may be won over without words by the behavior of their wives, when they see the purity and reverence of your lives."

USING OUR FAMILY TO INFLUENCE OTHERS

"We are therefore Christ's ambassadors, as though God were making his appeal through us." (2 Corinthians 5:20). What if God designed our family to reflect heaven on earth... something so unusual, beautiful, and attractive that the searching world stopped to ask how they too could have such love? Many young people under thirty years of age believe that it is very difficult or even impossible to have a good marriage today. That generation is asking big questions about marriage, and big questions about God. We are convinced one way that God desires to grab the attention of Millennials is through healthy, thriving, Christ-centered marriages and families. Ones so healthy and secure that they attract truth-seekers. Is our marriage full of life, filled with the love, support, affirmation, and respect, living each day joyfully and abundantly? Do we have a family that obviously enjoys being together, who treat one another with love and respect, who have fun? In no way do we expect our families to exist without conflict or pain, but to thrive despite circumstances because of the supernatural love found in our deep connection to Christ.

As we experience God-sized dreams for our marriages and families, we will be able to point others straight to Jesus. Christ will be on display and will draw people to him. People are watching our lives and asking: "Does having Jesus as Lord really mean anything in the daily life of Christians?" Imagine what could happen if the church were full of "heaven-on-earth" families that acted as beacons, clearly pointing to the power and majesty of Christ.

Without question, the relationships within our family are the greatest evangelism tool we have. On a beach, in a restaurant, on a plane, in a mall, it just happens. People notice that we love and enjoy one another and they see the way we treat each other. Sometimes they'll comment about it. Eventually they may get to the question: "What is your secret?" But, as important as our example is, most of the time we will have to find a way to initiate a conversation. The "how" depends on who we want to share with. If it is a stranger that we most likely will never see again, we need to seize the opportunity on the spot. If it is a friend, neighbor or work-associate, we probably need to use opportunities to build a relationship that can lead to natural conversations.

Building a soul-seeking heart in our kids is very important. As they grow in their awareness of the importance of having their own relationship with God, they need to be taught that God wants everyone to seek him. Their seeing us share our faith with others, seeing us studying the Bible with others, seeing baptisms, and hearing us praying for others will help them be inspired to share their faith with others. We remember times, when our girls were teenagers, that all five of us were involved in studying the Bible with others—what an encouraging time!

God created marriage to be much more that a perennial honeymoon that only two lovers enjoy. He intends for it to be a blessing to all who encounter it; for it to be a light that guides all who see it into an eternal relationship with the Father.

Chapter Twenty-Nine

RECOVER FROM MARRIAGE DISASTER

"Ah, Sovereign LORD, you have made the heavens and the earth by your great power and outstretched arm. Nothing is too hard for you."
—Jeremiah 32:17

Hopefully, not many of you will need this chapter for yourselves. If you do have a marriage on the brink of divorce, do not give up. If you have friends on the brink of divorce, encourage them not to give up. God specializes in miracles. It is never too late with God.

Very few things hurt as bad as a marriage that is falling apart, and there is no loneliness as intense as living with a stranger who used to be your best friend and lover. Then life is filled with pain, anguish, and disenchantment. But divorce statistics show "falling out of love" is very common, as about half of marriages end in divorce. It's a scary place to be, and sometimes it can seem like it came out of nowhere. The reality is, if you've reached the point where you feel like you are no longer "in love," or your marriage is dead, it's probably been happening over time; it didn't happen overnight.

There are several things we need in order to survive as humans: food, water, and air to name a few. Just like we need those essentials to survive physically, marriages need certain things to survive emotionally: things like love, trust, truth, patience, kindness, and understanding. When a marriage is missing these things, it can slowly (or quickly) die. And hope often dies with it. Can there be hope? Is it worth going on? We want to share a miracle story of a dead marriage being raised to life; just one of many we have witnessed through the years. But this miracle story is fresh; it happened shortly before Gloria passed.

James and Karen (not their real names, and a few facts have been changed to protect their privacy) are a striking, talented couple. Both graduated from the Air Force Academy and began their military careers. While they were stationed at the same base, they met, fell in love and moved in together. Because they were not married, their next assignments took them to different places half way around the world from one another. Before their next assignment, so they could be stationed together, they married, but that was after they had already been apart for a year. They then had a year together as husband and wife, however during that time, things fell apart. They separated, James quit the Air Force and moved across the country from Karen. They didn't see each other for almost two years. Each went separately to counseling. James' counselor advised him to get a divorce. During that time, he met a Christian who studied the Bible with him, and he became a disciple of Jesus. James, who still cared for Karen but had no desire to live with her, asked disciples who lived near her to invite her to church. She went, studied the Bible for several months, and was baptized.

Now they were both disciples who were married but had not seen each other in two years. Disciples in both places started encouraging them to pray and work towards getting back together. Karen was open to the idea, however James was terrified at the thought of going back into such a painful marriage. Christian friends continued to work with both separately. Finally, James had a breakthrough; he realized that as committed and reborn followers of Jesus they didn't have to go back to the way they were, because God is powerful enough to change them both. From then on, they made rapid progress in their relationship with each other. When they saw each other for the first time in two years it was like love at first sight. Shortly thereafter, they had a renewal of their vows with many people present who had worked and prayed so hard for their marriage. I (Al) asked James what was the "aha moment" for him in deciding to make the marriage work. What he said was profound, "I realized that marriage is not meant to make us happy, but to make us holy as we pursue God together."

You may want to stay together but feel that there is too much broken or wrong with your relationship to make that happen. It's not an easy thing to admit that things aren't going well. The good news is that you, as a follower of Jesus, have tools to get things back on track. For the remainder of the chapter we are going to discuss some of the necessary ingredients for turning things around. It is significant that what is needed to rebuild a marriage involves the same things that are needed to build a solid marriage in the first place.

ESSENTIALS BEFORE REBUILDING CAN START

Before we even talk about rebuilding, three marriage-killers must be removed: marital infidelity, physical abuse and drug or alcohol addiction. Infidelity can be overcome, but not unless the illicit relationship is totally ended, and there is godly sorrow for the adultery. Physical abuse cannot be tolerated at all. And we have found that any type of drug or alcohol addiction that is not being treated will prevent any real progress in rebuilding the marriage.

REBUILD THE FOUNDATION

God is the rebuilder of marriage, and he is the only one who can do it so that it will last. Satan has sold society the lie that tells us that we get married to be happy for the rest of our lives, and that our spouse is responsible for making us happy. When this doesn't happen, we can become bitter, angry and disillusioned because our expectations aren't met. This is not at all how God designed marriage to work. But, is there any way to get back to the love you once knew? The answer is absolutely YES! The God who raised Jesus from the dead can breathe life into your dead and decaying marriage. That doesn't mean it will be easy. In fact, it may be the hardest thing you have ever done, but it will be worth it.

To rebuild the marriage foundation, you first need to examine your own personal foundation with God. How is your relationship with him; do you really depend on him? Are you reading your Bible and praying every day? Are you actively involved in the body-life of his church? Are the two of you praying together every day? It is going to take a dependence on God for the two of you like you have never had before. This means that you must recognize that you are not in control, but that God is. He must be the focus of your life, not you, not your mate, not your career, not money, nor kids, but God. Remember what James realized about marriage that was the turning point for him—marriage is not meant to make us happy, but to make us holy as we pursue God together.

FOCUS ON CHANGING YOURSELF, NOT YOUR MATE

"But if he would just change... then I'd feel so much happier or more loved." Sound familiar? It is very harmful to a relationship to pressure your mate to change. This kind of thinking doesn't work for two reasons: First, you can't change someone else. You can only change yourself. Secondly, trying to change your spouse will create tension in your relationship and probably discourage him or her from changing. And even if your mate did change, he or she wouldn't feel very good about the relationship until you made some changes yourself. Rebuilding your marriage begins with you being willing to examine your own part in your marriage troubles and becoming a better partner yourself.

FORGIVE

When your marriage is broken, healing will not take place without a lot of forgiveness. The first step is to get in touch with the things that you hold against your mate. There may be a long list. Perhaps, even some of the things you initially found attractive have become irritants. You need to take each of those things to God and ask him for the strength to let go of the bitterness and truly forgive. Let your mate know what you have forgiven them for. Next, you need to get in touch with the things that your mate holds against you. Ask God to make you aware of the ways you have hurt your mate and to give you humility to sincerely apologize. Ask God to give you the empathy for your spouse that you need to understand how those hurts have harmed your marriage. Listen to your partner's version of the hurt, without getting defensive. Ask them to forgive you and let them know that you are going to really try to change.

BE THANKFUL

Get back to basics and remember what is was like when you were first together and first in love. Think about what made you both fall in love with one another. Think about what you admired about this person and what made you want to be with them. Be thankful for all the great times you have had together. Be thankful that you are still together and that you still have the chance to rebuild the marriage. Most of all, be thankful that Almighty God is at work helping you to work towards building the kind of marriage that he wants us all to have. Journaling will often help. Maybe walking and praying daily. Take some tangible steps to cultivate the kind of relationship that married couples need so they can build new habits together.

GET HELP

Look for support from your church community. Look for a couple who cares about the two of you, and ask them to pray for you, and mentor you as you work to reconcile. Accept help from family, friends, your church leaders, and others for whatever you need. Find a disciple of the same sex who you can become accountable to. Be open and honest with them. Seek Christian counseling if needed.

Remember, God is for you, and he can see beyond the present, when you can't. He is good all the time, even when your marriage and life seem to be falling apart. He is for you and wants you to have a great marriage. And remember, it's not over until it is over.

FINISHING THE RACE

*"I have fought the good fight, I have
finished the race, I have kept the faith."*
—2 Timothy 4:7

On July 14, 2018 Gloria went home to be with God, and I really miss her. Our fifty-six years of marriage has moved to a new phase. She is in paradise and now we have a long-distance relationship. She bravely fought cancer full of joy and without complaining for six years. She is absolutely the toughest person I have ever known. In the month prior to her death, she had gotten progressively weaker and had fallen several times. Her oncologist ordered a brain scan and called me the evening of the scan with the news that the cancer had progressed to her brain. We met with him, and he told us that the end was near. I later found a text on her phone that she had sent to some of her close friends, "Dr says he thinks I have weeks not months... so Heaven here I come!!!! Don't like saying goodbye!!! Love you sooo much! Keep fighting the fight!!" Twelve days later she was gone.

Those twelve days were some of the most special ones of our life. All our girls, their husbands and our grandkids came; we laughed, cried, sang and prayed. Gloria always had a great sense of humor, but she took it to a whole new level. At one point when we were expecting her to pass at any moment, she called me in and said, "I think this may be the end... but I don't know because I've never done this before!" And one by one, she had a parting talk with each of the grandkids and gave them her challenge for them. If we had designed the perfect end to her life, we could not have done nearly as well as God did.

As we grew older, we talked about how we would like the end to come. Our wish was to go together, but we knew that wasn't likely. So, we jokingly argued about who would get to go first, because neither of us wanted to be left behind. She won. I never imagined how hard it would be to lose my best friend and lover and to figure out life from here.

We were married in a hurricane on September 11, 1961. (Yes, 9/11 is our anniversary). September 11, 2018 would have been our fifty-seventh anniversary, so I decided to celebrate with her in spirit at our favorite get-away bed-and-breakfast in Dana Point, California on our anniversary. When we were dating, we were apart for two summers, and we wrote each other every day. We had saved all of those more than three hundred letters from fifty-seven years ago, and we had never gone back and reread them. I decided to take all those letters with me to Dana Point and read them. I read and laughed and cried for fifteen hours over two days (many of the letters were ten pages long). It was an incredibly moving experience, because it was just like talking with Gloria fifty-seven years ago! Many times since losing her, I have wished that I had just one more day with her and this was like God gave me, not one, but two days with her.

We had both decided to be cremated. When I got her ashes, I kept them in the bedroom with me until I decided where to scatter them. Initially I was going to spread them at our favorite get-away spot in Dana Point, but then I kept thinking of more and more special spots. So far, I have spread them in nine different places that hold very special memories for the two of us. That way, when I think of those special memories, I can know that a little of her is still there. There are other places that I am hoping for, but we'll see what happens as some are far away outside of the USA.

I never even considered getting a tattoo, but after she passed, I decided that I wanted one that would remind me of her. For years I had drawn a heart with an arrow through it and her initials on every card that I gave her. That is what I wanted for my tattoo. My granddaughter, who is an accomplished artist and is branching into tattoo art, designed it. I had it inked on the inside of my wrist, and it is a great comfort to me.

When our first grandchild was born, Gloria started a "birthstone baby" necklace. As each of our nine grandchildren were born, she added a piece with their birthstone on it. All the kids wanted theirs after Gloria passed, so we gave theirs to them on their own necklace.

When we were married, we marveled at all the "firsts." Our first time making love, our first apartment, our first Christmas together, etc. These were so exciting. Now I have a whole new set of firsts. My first night alone in our king-size bed, my first meal alone, the first time going back to church without her, my first Christmas without her, our first anniversary without her, and so many other firsts that are yet to come. These firsts are not exciting, but painful. I keep forgetting that she is gone; everything is still "we" in my thinking. Several times a day I think of something to ask her or tell her and then I remember shc is gone. When I am out, I see couples holding hands and I envy them. On one walk, I said "hello" to a guy walking his dog passing in the other direction. A few seconds later, he said "What are you doing alone?" I heard some else respond, and realized he was not talking to me, but it cut like a knife because my life is now lived being alone. Most of the songs I hear remind me of her. In fact, there is not much that doesn't remind me of her.

I talk to everyone I know who has lost a mate to learn from them how they have successfully grieved their loss. When your mate dies, you grieve not only the loss of the person, but also for the life you used to have, the love the person gave you and all the special times you spent together. One friend who had lost her husband several years ago said that things still occasionally happen that feel like "paper cuts." The pain is not as intense as it was at first, but it still stings for a little while. Another friend said that a good response to someone asking how you are doing is to say, "I'm okay, but I'm not okay; and that is okay."

I suppose that all of this seems very heavy; but I purposely have included it because in running the marriage race together, one of you will probably cross the finish line before the other. It is a part of life that we need to live victoriously. It is very painful to lose your mate, but it is a "good" pain filled with incredible memories. Gloria faced her death with faith, love, and courage. There will never be another person as beautiful and amazing to me inside and out as she was. On a scale of 1-10 she was a 12. Hopefully, you feel that way about your mate.

My challenge now is to live as well as she died. I don't want to "get over" her. One of Gloria's favorite verses was Psalms 31:14-15, "*But I trust in you, O Lord; I say 'You are my God.' My times are in your hands...*" It is important that we live trusting that our times are in God's hands. I believe that God knew what he was doing in taking Gloria first. That means that he has more for me to do than sit around feeling sorry for myself. Our lives have been filled with amazing adventures for fifty-six years; and I have a hunch that there are more exciting adventures ahead for me, for however much time he gives me.

The "paper cuts" will probably continue, but God also continues his showers of blessings. He recently helped me "rediscover" a passage that I knew, but that now has taken on new meaning: 1 Thessalonians 4:13, where Paul writes, "*we do not want you to be uninformed about those who sleep in death, so that you do not grieve like the rest of mankind, who have no hope.*" He goes on to say that when Jesus returns at the end of time, the dead in Christ will be raised and those faithful who are still alive will join them. And they will be together with God forever! So now when I take communion alone, celebrating Jesus' death, burial and resurrection, it is with a new hope and realization that Gloria and I will be together again. The tearful goodbyes at her passing have been replaced with an excited "See you later!" Now, I just need to make sure that I am a faithful disciple to the end.

Resources for Christian Growth from Illumination Publishers

Apologetics

Compelling Evidence for God and the Bible—Truth in an Age of Doubt, by Douglas Jacoby.
Field Manual for Christian Apologetics, by John M. Oakes.
Is There A God—Questions and Answers about Science and the Bible, by John M. Oakes.
Mormonism—What Do the Evidence and Testimony Reveal?, by John M. Oakes.
Reasons For Belief–A Handbook of Christian Evidence, by John M. Oakes.
That You May Believe—Reflections on Science and Jesus, by John Oakes/David Eastman.
The Resurrection: A Historical Analysis, by C. Foster Stanback.
When God Is Silent—The Problem of Human Suffering, by Douglas Jacoby.

Bible Basics

A Disciple's Handbook—Third Edition, Tom A. Jones, Editor.
A Quick Overview of the Bible, by Douglas Jacoby.
Be Still, My Soul—A Practical Guide to a Deeper Relationship with God, by Sam Laing.
From Shadow to Reality—Relationship of the Old & New Testament, by John M. Oakes.
Getting the Most from the Bible, Second Edition, by G. Steve Kinnard.
Letters to New Disciples—Practical Advice for New Followers of Jesus, by Tom A. Jones.
The Baptized Life—The Lifelong Meaning of Immersion into Christ, by Tom A. Jones.
The Lion Never Sleeps—Preparing Those You Love for Satans Attacks, by Mike Taliaferro.
The New Christian's Field Guide, Joseph Dindinger, Editor.
Thirty Days at the Foot of the Cross, Tom and Sheila Jones, Editors.

Christian Living

According to Your Faith—The Awesome Power of Belief in God, by Richard Alawaye
But What About Your Anger—A Biblical Guide to Managing Your Anger, by Lee Boger.
Caring Beyond the Margins—Understanding Homosexuality, by Guy Hammond.
Golden Rule Membership—What God Expects of Every Disciple, by John M. Oakes.
How to Defeat Temptation in Under 60 Seconds, by Guy Hammond.
Jesus and the Poor—Embracing the Ministry of Jesus, by G. Steve Kinnard.
How to Be a Missionary in Your Hometown, by Joel Nagel.
Like a Tree Planted by Streams of Water—Personal Spiritual Growth, G. Steve Kinnard.
Love One Another—Importance & Power of Christian Relationships, by Gordon Ferguson.
One Another—Transformational Relationships, by Tom A. Jones and Steve Brown.
Prepared to Answer—Restoring Truth in An Age of Relativism, by Gordon Ferguson.
Repentance—A Cosmic Shift of Mind & Heart, by Edward J. Anton.
Strong in the Grace—Reclaiming the Heart of the Gospel, by Tom A. Jones.
The Guilty Soul's Guide to Grace—Freedom in Christ, by Sam Laing.
The Power of Discipling, by Gordon Ferguson.
The Prideful Soul's Guide to Humility, by Tom A. Jones and Michael Fontenot.
The Way of the Heart—Spiritual Living in a Legalistic World, by G. Steve Kinnard.
The Way of the Heart of Jesus—Prayer, Fasting, Bible Study, by G. Steve Kinnard.
Till the Nets Are Full—An Evangelism Handbook for the 21st Century, by Douglas Jacoby.
Walking the Way of the Heart—Lessons for Spiritual Living, by G. Steve Kinnard.
Values and Habits of Spiritual Growth, by Bryan Gray.

Deeper Study

A Women's Ministry Handbook, by Jennifer Lambert and Kay McKean.

After The Storm—Hope & Healing From Ezra—Nehemiah, by Rolan Dia Monje.

Aliens and Strangers—The Life and Letters of Peter, by Brett Kreider.

Crossing the Line: Culture, Race, and Kingdom, by Michael Burns.

Daniel—Prophet to the Nations, by John M. Oakes.

Exodus—Making Israel's Journey Your Own, by Rolan Dia Monje.

Exodus—Night of Redemption, by Douglas Jacoby.

Finish Strong—The Message of Haggai, Zechariah, and Malachi, by Rolan Dia Monje.

In Remembrance of Me—Understanding the Lord's Supper, by Andrew C. Fleming.

In the Middle of It!—Tools to Help Preteen and Young Teens, by Jeff Rorabaugh.

Into the Psalms—Verses for the Heart, Music for the Soul, by Rolan Dia Monje.

King Jesus—A Survey of the Life of Jesus the Messiah, by G. Steve Kinnard.

Jesus Unequaled—An Exposition of Colossians, by G. Steve Kinnard.

Passport to the Land of Enough—Revised Edition, by Joel Nagel.

Prophets I—The Voices of Yahweh, by G. Steve Kinnard

Prophets II—The Prophets of the Assyrian Period, by G. Steve Kinnard

Prophets III—The Prophets of the Babylonian and Persion Periods, by G. Steve Kinnard.

Return to Sender—When There's Nowhere Left to Go but Home, by Guy Hammond.

Romans—The Heart Set Free, by Gordon Ferguson.

Revelation Revealed—Keys to Unlocking the Mysteries of Revelation, by Gordon Ferguson.

Spiritual Leadership for Women, Jeanie Shaw, Editor.

The Call of the Wise—An Introduction and Index of Proverbs, by G. Steve Kinnard.

The Cross of the Savior—From the Perspective of Jesus..., by Mark Templer.

The Final Act—A Biblical Look at End-Time Prophecy, by G. Steve Kinnard.

The Gospel of Matthew—The Crowning of the King, by G. Steve Kinnard.

The Letters of James, Peter, John, Jude—Life to the Full, by Douglas Jacoby.

The Lion Has Roared—An Exposition of Amos, by Douglas Jacoby.

The Seven People Who Help You to Heaven, by Sam Laing.

The Spirit—Presense & Power, Sense & Nonsense, by Douglas Jacoby.

Thrive—Using Psalms to Help You Flourish, by Douglas Jacoby.

What Happens After We Die?, by Dr. Douglas Jacoby.

World Changers—The History of the Church in the Book of Acts, by Gordon Ferguson.

Marriage and Family

Building Emotional Intimacy in Your Marriage, by Jeff and Florence Schachinger.

Hot and Holy—God's Plan for Exciting Sexual Intimacy in Marriage, by Sam Laing.

Faith and Finances, by Patrick Blair.

Friends & Lovers—Marriage as God Designed It, by Sam and Geri Laing.

Mighty Man of God—A Return to the Glory of Manhood, by Sam Laing.

Raising Awesome Kids—Being the Great Influence in Your Kids' Lives by Sam and Geri Laing.

Principle-Centered Parenting, by Douglas and Vicki Jacoby.

The Essential 8 Principles of a Growing Christian Marriage, by Sam and Geri Laing.

The Essential 8 Principles of a Strong Family, by Sam and Geri Laing.

Warrior—A Call to Every Man Everywhere, by Sam Laing.

All these and more available at www.ipibooks.com

Books
available
from
www.ipibooks.com

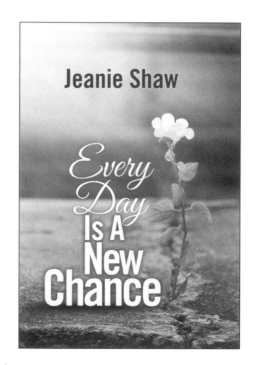

Books
available
from
www.ipibooks.com

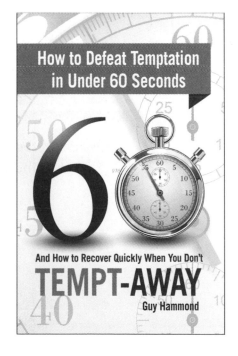

For additional books go to
www.ipibooks.com